Study Skills for PTLLS

Study Skills for PTLLS

Jacklyn Williams
Editor: Ann Gravells

2nd edition

Los Angeles | London | New Delhi
Singapore | Washington DC

Learning Matters
An imprint of SAGE Publications Ltd
I Oliver's Yard
55 City Road
London
ECIY ISP

SAGE Publications Inc
2455 Teller Road
Thousand Oaks, California 91320

SAGE Publications India PVT LTD
BI/I I Mohan Cooperative Industrial Area
Malthura Road
New Dehli 110 044

SAGE Publications Asia-Pacific Pte Ltd
3 Church Street
#10–04 Samsung Hub
Singapore 049483

Editor: Amy Thornton
Development Editor: Jennifer Clark
Production Controller: Chris Marke
Project Management: Deer Park Productions, Tavistock
Marketing Manager: Catherine Slinn
Cover Design: Topics
Typeset by: Pantek Media
Printed by: TJ International Ltd, Padstow, Cornwall

Library of Congress Control Number:
2012936243

British Library Cataloguing in Publication data

A catalogue record for this book is available from the British Library

ISBN: 978 0 85725 693 0
ISBN: 978 0 85725 887 8 (pbk)

MIX
Paper from
responsible sources
FSC
www.fsc.org   FSC® C013056

CONTENTS

ACKNOWLEDGEMENTS

I would like to thank the following for their patience, encouragement and support while writing the second edition of this book.

Hilary Allen
Jennifer Clark
Di Dawson
Ann Gravells
Amy Thornton
Christopher Williams
Helen Williams
Max Williams

Every effort has been made to trace the copyright holders and to obtain their permission for the use of copyright material. The publisher and author will gladly receive any information enabling them to rectify any error or omission in subsequent editions.

Jacklyn Williams has been teaching since 1995, developing, managing and teaching post-compulsory education programmes in Business, Education, Key Skills, Leadership and Management, Skills for Life and Teacher Education. She has worked across sectors including higher and further education, personal and community development learning, family learning, the prison service, and work-based learning.

Jacklyn is director and owner of Paramount Progressive Solutions Limited, an educational consultancy specialising in teaching and training in lifelong learning. She is also an NLP Master Practitioner, which she says brings an added dimension to all her work.

Jacklyn holds an MA in Education, together with specialist qualifications in teacher education, coaching and mentoring, dyslexia and literacy, ESOL, numeracy and e-learning. She is a Fellow of the Institute for Learning and has QTLS status. Jacklyn can be contacted via her website: www.prosolteaching. co.uk

As a teacher of the PTLLS Award I know how some students struggle with their studies, not only with note-taking, research and referencing, but managing their busy lives to complete the formal assessment requirements. As the PTLLS Award is four units on the Qualifications and Credit Framework, it requires you to study in your own time to support your learning. Knowing how to use this time effectively for self-study is a skill all of its own.

This second edition has been fully updated to include a chapter regarding reflective practice, along with further information regarding referencing your work.

This book will help you understand how to approach the PTLLS Award assessment requirements by giving you advice on how to study effectively, carry out research, write in an academic style and reference your work.

I hope this book, and the others in the PTLLS series, will help you pass your PTLLS Award and begin a rewarding career in teaching in the Lifelong Learning Sector.

Ann Gravells
www.anngravells.co.uk

The structure of the book and how to use it

The purpose of the book

The book has been specifically written for anyone who is working towards the Preparing to Teach in the Lifelong Learning Sector (PTLLS) Award at either level 3 or level 4. You might not yet be teaching (known as pre-service), but are hoping to embark on a career in post-compulsory teaching or training – known as the Lifelong Learning Sector. Or you might already be an experienced teacher (known as in-service), who needs to obtain a suitable teaching qualification. You might be returning to study after a long break, or be taking the PTLLS Award alongside another qualification. The book has therefore been designed to provide an easy-to-use guide to the academic skills needed to:

- use study time efficiently

- develop effective learning strategies

- work towards meeting the PTLLS Award learning outcomes and assessment criteria

The book is intended to take you on a journey from when you commence your PTLLS Award (or even before, while you consider whether it is right for you), through the various stages of gaining the skills, knowledge and understanding needed to meet deadlines and produce the required work in a well-organised, attractively presented portfolio.

Even if you decide that you do not wish to complete the PTLLS Award at this stage, the information in the book will prove invaluable in guiding you through a range of strategies to enable you to study and learn more effectively.

Content and structure

The book is confined to study skills relevant to the PTLLS Award, the information in it being complementary to that in the companion textbooks by Ann Gravells, *Preparing to Teach in the Lifelong Learning Sector* and *Passing PTLLS Assessments*. These texts give specific information relating to the full process of teaching along with guidance to help you demonstrate and evidence your competence.

Each chapter contains activities to enable you to engage with the content and identify its relevance to your own situation; there are also examples to help your understanding. At the end of each chapter is a list of textbooks, websites and other resources which will enable you to research relevant topics further.

For ease and speed of understanding, abbreviations and acronyms are expanded the first time that they are used in each chapter. This is something that you would also do within your own written work.

The appendices include answers to the formal activities in the chapters together with a list of useful books and websites.

The index will help you quickly locate topics if you are dipping into the book to find specific information, or want to check up on a particular point. Again, this is something you can do with any textbook to help you quickly find the information you need.

How to use the book

Each chapter stands alone and can be read independently. You may choose to read consecutively from Chapter 1 to Chapter 7, or to work through the chapters according to your requirements at the time. Alternatively, you may decide to use the book as a reference source and look up relevant aspects within the chapters as required.

The PTLLS Award can be studied in many different ways; for example, face-to-face, distance learning, and/or blended learning. It is delivered over varying time spans, from intensive one-week programmes to day or evening classes lasting ten weeks or more. Accreditation is through many different Awarding Organisations, each with their own assessment strategy. The content of the qualification is the same; however, it can be assessed differently as long as all the assessment criteria are met during the process. The PTLLS Award can be completed as a stand-alone qualification, or as part of the Certificate (CTLLS) or the Diploma (DTLLS) in Teaching in the Lifelong Learning Sector; the latter is also known as the Certificate in Education (Cert. Ed.) or Post Graduate Certificate in Education (PGCE).

Whichever route you follow to achieve your PTLLS Award, the study skills needed for successful completion will be the same. This book has been organised so that the necessary skills are presented in a way that is useful and accessible to anyone following any PTLLS Award programme.

The book should fully meet your requirements whether you are completing the PTLLS Award at level 3 or level 4, as you can pick and mix the pages that you study according to your needs at the time. If you are aiming to achieve at level 3, you might choose not to go into too much detail regarding research and referencing. If you are aiming to achieve at level 4, you will need to carry out independent research and write in an academic style, referencing your work to theorists. You will therefore find the chapter on this topic particularly useful. Your assessor will be able to inform you of any particular awarding organisation requirements.

Whatever your journey towards your qualification, and whether the PTLLS Award is the final stop for you or a platform on which to build, this is the beginning of a journey to an enjoyable, rewarding and worthwhile career.

Theory focus

Books

Gravells, A. (2012a) *Preparing to Teach in the Lifelong Learning Sector*, (5th Edn.) London: Learning Matters.

Gravells, A. (2012b) *Passing PTLLS Assessments*, (2nd Edn.) London: Learning Matters.

LLUK (2006) *New overarching professional standards for teachers, tutors and trainers in the Lifelong Learning Sector*. London: LLUK.

Websites

Department for Business, Innovation and Skills	www.bis.gov.uk
Gravells, A.	www.anngravells.co.uk
Learning and Skills Improvement Service	www.lsis.org.uk

Introduction

In this chapter you will learn about:

- meeting the Lifelong Learning professional teaching standards
- interpreting the skills needed for the PTLLS Award
- becoming an expert learner

There are activities and examples to help you reflect on the above which will assist your understanding of how to prepare for your PTLLS Award.

Meeting the Lifelong Learning professional teaching standards

In 2007, new regulations in England introduced professional teaching standards with licensed practitioner status for all new teachers of government-funded programmes in the Lifelong Learning Sector. This includes all post-16 education, including further education, adult and community learning, work-based learning and offender education. Full details of the standards can be accessed at www.education.gov.uk/publications/standard/publication Detail/Page1/LLUK-00559-2007.

The Award in Preparing to Teach in the Lifelong Learning Sector (PTLLS) is the first stage of the qualifications which were produced from the teaching standards. It is a four-unit Award on the Qualifications and Credit Framework (QCF), and provides an entry point and introduction for those new to teaching or those wishing to teach.

If you are currently employed as a teacher, or wish to teach, the teaching you undertake will be classed as one of two distinct roles:

- An associate teaching role which involves fewer teaching responsibilities and requires Associate Teacher Learning and Skills (ATLS) status.

- A full teaching role which includes the complete scope of teaching responsibilities and requires Qualified Teacher Learning and Skills (QTLS) status.

You will need to obtain your professional teaching status within five years of commencing your role, and the PTLLS Award is the first step towards achieving the relevant teaching qualifications. You will also need to register with the Institute for Learning (IfL), the professional body for teachers in the Lifelong Learning Sector.

This book was written prior to the Lord Lingfield Interim Report *Professionalism in Further Education* (2012). There may have been some changes to the requirements for teachers in the Lifelong Learning Sector as a result of the subsequent report which was due after this book was published.

The PTLLS Award

PTLLS is a four-unit Award on the Qualifications and Credit Framework (QCF) which has a credit value of 12, this means it takes approximately 120 hours to achieve. This will be a mixture of contact time with a tutor/ assessor and non-contact time for self-study. Achievement of the units provides an entry point and introduction for those new to teaching or those wishing to teach. The PTLLS Award can also be embedded into the first part of the *Certificate in Teaching in the Lifelong Learning Sector* (CTLLS – 24 credits) or the *Diploma in Teaching in the Lifelong Learning Sector* (DTLLS – 120 credits). The latter is also known as the Certificate in Education (Cert Ed) or the Postgraduate Certificate in Education (PGCE).

The PTLLS Award is made up of the following four units available at both level 3 and 4 or their *accepted alternatives*.

- Roles, responsibilities and relationships in lifelong learning

- Understanding inclusive learning and teaching in lifelong learning

- Using inclusive learning and teaching approaches in lifelong learning

- Principles of assessment in lifelong learning

Accepted alternatives come from the Learning and Development qualification. For example, if you have already achieved the unit *Understanding the principles and practices of assessment* you could use it as an alternative to *Principles of assessment in lifelong learning*. However, there are rules as to which units can be used instead of those above.

The accepted alternative units are:

● Facilitate learning and development for individuals

● Facilitate learning and development in groups

● Manage learning and development in groups

● Understanding the principles and practices of assessment

The PTLLS Award is offered at two levels to allow for differentiation. For example, if you are taking level 3 you will *explain* how or why you do something, at level 4 you will *analyse* how or why you do it. Your teacher will be able to give you guidance regarding the levels and the amount of work you will need to submit. Besides preparing and delivering a micro teach session, you will need to submit evidence of your achievements which might take the form of:

● action plan

● assessment grid and checklist

● assignment

● essay

● observation checklist

● online assessment

● peer feedback

● practical task

● professional discussion

● reflective learning journal

● responses to questions

● self-evaluation record

● summative profile

● theory task

● worksheet

Your assessor will be able to give you the specific assessment requirements for the level you are taking. You will also find information about the various assessment methods and Awarding Organisations' requirements in the companion textbook by Ann Gravells, *Passing PTLLS assessments*. Whichever form of assessment tasks you complete, you should submit them in a folder known as a portfolio, either electronically or manually depending upon the requirements.

PTLLS Award requirements at level 3

At level 3 your work needs to be attractively presented, logically structured, free from error, and should describe relevant methods and activities. Sometimes you will also need to include justification; for example, explaining why and how you did something. For more information about the meanings of terms used in assessment questions, see Chapter 6. It is also good practice to include a record of wider reading in a bibliography. A bibliography is a list of books, journals, etc. that have been accessed during the study process, but have not been directly quoted from within your writing.

Activity

Think about how you would approach your response to a written assessment task at level 3. Make a list of everything you think it should have/do and also those things that it definitely should not have/should do. Here are a few suggestions to get you started.

PTLLS level 3 written assessments

Should have/do:	Should not have/do:
Full question stated at the top of the page	*Spelling errors*
Double- or one-and-a-half-line spacing	*Mistakes in grammar*

When you have finished, look at Appendix 1 to see how many aspects you have identified. Refer to this list when you are working towards your assessments.

PTLLS Award requirements at level 4

At level 4, your assessment content needs to move beyond describing and justifying, to include an element of evaluation; for example, identifying strengths and areas for development, advantages and limitations. For more information about the meanings of terms used in assessment questions, see Chapter 6. You also need to carry out independent research and use citations (paraphrasing another author's work) or insert direct quotations from books and internet sites to support your arguments. Your work will need to show that you:

- understand the relationship between theories, principles and practice, and the relevance of this in your own teaching context

- have considered how professional values relate to, and impact on, your role, responsibilities and boundaries as a teacher

- can plan effectively and write focused and concise responses

- can write in an academic style, using a recognised system of referencing (the Harvard system is recommended, which is explained in Chapter 5)

Activity

Think about how you would approach your response to a written assessment task at level 4. Make a list of everything you think it should have/do, and also those things that it definitely should not *have/do. If you have already completed this activity for level 3, you can add the extra requirements for level 4. Here are a few suggestions to get you started.*

PTLLS level 4 written assessments

Should have/do:	Should not have/do:
Full question stated at the top of the page	*Spelling errors*
Double- or one-and-a-half-line spacing	*Mistakes in grammar*
...	*...*
Use of complete sentences with only minor use of bullets and tables	*Use of inappropriate references which have no evidence of origin or authenticity (known as provenance)*

When you have finished, look at Appendix 1 to see how many aspects you have identified. Refer to this list when you are working towards your assessments.

Interpreting the skills needed for the PTLLS Award

In order to complete your PTLLS Award, you will need to use a range of skills including planning, organisation, research and communication. Essential planning and organisational skills are explained opposite. Aspects of undertaking research and spoken and written communication are discussed in detail in Chapters 3 and 6.

Planning

To be able to study effectively requires advance planning. You will need to establish the amount of time you have available for study and try to schedule this into the hours when you have most mental and physical energy. Study time is often wasted because people attempt to start, or keep working on tasks when they are tired. If you start to feel overwhelmed and overtired, or hungry, it is time to stop and sleep, eat, or take some light exercise such as going for a short walk. These activities will help to recharge your energy levels, and although they might seem to be wasting precious time, they will enable you to get two or three times as much work done, of a much higher quality, when you restart.

The following guidelines should help you to establish effective study patterns.

- Work out how much time you are able to set aside for study.

- Once you have established a time allowance, think about whether you can establish a regular allotted time, or whether your study times have to be flexible to fit in with other commitments.

- Get into a routine early on.

- Little and often is better than long periods of continuous study. Try to divide your study time into short, manageable blocks; for example,
  - work for about 20 minutes
  - break for 3–4 minutes to actively review what you have done
  - work for another 20 minutes
  - break for 3–4 minutes to review
  - rest, and enjoy a small reward: a piece of fruit, a drink, or a short walk
  - move on to the next topic, or stop

- Always attend sessions on time unless there is a real emergency.

- Communicate with your teacher/assessor regularly.

- Make a note of all your assessment deadlines on a wall planner that is easily visible when you are working.

Organisation of your working environment

Set up your work area so that it is comfortable, attractive and conducive to working. Make sure that you have a comfortable chair that supports your back and allows your feet to sit flat on the floor. Have a bottle of water to hand, and try to ensure you have a pleasant aspect: a view through a window, a plant, or an attractive picture if possible.

Before you start, identify a specific task to complete, and tidy your workspace, leaving only that task in front of you. Gather all the information you need to complete it: assessment criteria, textbooks, references lists, notes, papers, work materials, writing materials, computer storage devices, access codes, email addresses, etc. Lay them out in the order in which you will need to use them, so that they can easily be reached.

Ensure your clock or watch is easily visible, and settle down to work within your allocated time frame.

Becoming an expert learner

Characteristics

You might already have many skills of an expert learner. Some of these could have been developed from previous study, others from work, an interest or a hobby.

Activity

What characteristics do you think are necessary to become an expert learner? Write these on a separate piece of paper. When you have finished, compare your list with the one that follows but don't look yet.

An expert learner is:

- well organised
- able to plan, and think ahead
- good at time management, planning for, and working to, deadlines
- able to learn from mistakes
- able to understand programme requirements
- confident
- aware of own learning styles and preferences
- adaptable

- flexible

- able to work independently

- prepared to ask for help when necessary

- well motivated and self-directed

- curious

- a risk-taker

- resilient

- an advocate for themselves and others

- a good team-worker

- a negotiator

- able to think reflectively (about the past and the present)

- able to use correct spelling, grammar and punctuation

- able to analyse, evaluate and solve problems creatively

If you are faced with a challenging situation, you can adopt the *Achiever's* eight-step guide to creative problem-solving (Williams, 2010).

- **A**pproach the situation assuming there is a logical, workable solution.

- **C**hange to positive language; focus on what you want, not what you don't want.

- **H**ighlight all significant facts in writing.

- **I**temise all the possible causes of the situation; test out these causes.

- **E**stablish and itemise all possible solutions. (Don't pre-judge or evaluate yet.)

- **V**erify the best possible solution; now is the time to evaluate and make decisions.

- **E**nact – do it!

- **R**eview. Is the outcome satisfactory? Do you need to do something more?

Learning styles

Learning styles relate to a person's preferences for receiving information and problem-solving. Being aware of your learning style will help you to get the most out of learning opportunities and to identify areas for personal and professional development.

Perhaps the most widely-used learning styles model is VAK (visual, auditory, kinaesthetic), or learning through seeing, hearing and/or doing. If you don't already know your learning styles, access one of the websites listed at the end of this chapter and complete a questionnaire. Once you know your learning preference, you can adapt information and materials either to complement your strengths or to develop less preferred styles.

Activity

Now you have identified your learning preferences, take a few moments to think how you could make use of this information to:

a. adapt learning material to make it easier for you to understand and learn;

b. develop strengths where your skills are less well established.

Look at the following checklist and tick the things you feel you do well. Are there items on the list that you would like to include as personal goals for development? What about anything that is not on the list, but that you might like to add?

	Do well	Could improve
Visual/seeing		
Reviewing an activity by looking at something in print.		
Checking your notes are copied down accurately.		
Being sure to use upper and lower case letters (rather than capitals) and looking at the shapes/patterns that they make.		
Looking for words within words; for example, **format**ive.		
Using illustrations, charts and diagrams.		
Using highlighters to emphasise important points.		
Creating spray diagrams, spider diagrams, or concept maps.		
Turning your notes into a storyboard or cartoon strip.		
Finding pictures that support or replace text.		

Auditory/hearing		
Listening to tapes, podcasts, compact discs, to help you learn.		
Paraphrasing new learning to explain it in your own words.		
Discussing your ideas with peers or friends and family.		
Creating your own podcast explaining new information.		
Repeating words or phrases silently to yourself.		
Splitting words or phrases into syllables or chunks and exaggerating the sounds.		
Chanting words and phrases to music.		
Making rhymes from information you need to remember.		
Using active listening skills including questioning and summarising.		
Kinaesthetic/doing		
Carrying out a practical activity to review learning.		
Writing things out as a step-by-step account.		
Producing a written account paraphrasing new learning into your own words.		
Turning your notes into a storyboard or cartoon strip.		
Finger-tracing keywords while saying them out loud.		
Writing down key information from memory.		
Using joined-up writing, rather than printing to help with flow.		
Typing or word processing to increase speed and help with flow.		

VAK is only one learning styles model. The BBC, in conjunction with the Open University, offers a model that adds two further processes of feeling/belonging and reflecting/evaluating. Fleming's (2005) VARK model adds a read/write process. Honey and Mumford (1992) identify four different styles of reflectors, theorists, activists and pragmatists, while Gardner's (1983) multiple intelligence theory recognises eight different intelligences, namely:

- verbal/linguistic – an ability with words and language

- mathematical/logical – an aptitude for logic, reasoning and mathematical tasks

- musical – an aptitude for music, rhythm and composition

- inter-personal – a capacity for empathy and social awareness and involvement

- intra-personal – reflective and self-aware, an ability for personal organisation

- visual-spatial – an ability to think three-dimensionally and judge spatial relationships

- kinaesthetic – a capacity for dexterity and a keen sense of body awareness

- naturalist – an ability to recognise and categorise environmental elements, an affinity with nature

Today, many people accept both the idea and the importance of learning styles, and many different learning style models, instruments, quizzes and questionnaires exist. Coffield et al. identified 71 learning style models in their study published in 2004, although some have been little tested, and others are variations on a theme (Coffield et al., 2004). Not surprisingly, there is also much discussion about the reliability of these tools and the potential effectiveness of tailoring teaching and learning to them. This latter concern increases when reminded that in addition to the variety already identified, *the learning styles field is not unified, but instead is divided into three linked areas of activity: theoretical, pedagogical and commercial* (Coffield et al., 2004:1). Furthermore, there is widespread acknowledgement that learners' preferred styles are not fixed over time, or even perhaps at a single snapshot in time. (This is an experiment you might like to undertake yourself, working through your chosen learning styles questionnaire from time to time and saving and comparing the results.) Individual learning styles will quite possibly also vary according to the subject being studied; familiarity and confidence with it; interest level; and a myriad of other factors. In their study, Coffield et al. (2004) undertook an in-depth examination of 13 of the most influential learning style models from the 71 identified, and concluded that the reliability of many was in question. What mattered most, they concluded, was to match teaching not with individual preferences, but with the nature of the subject by providing appropriate teaching and learning methods, strategies, and context (Coffield et al., 2004).

However, a more recent study by the University of Pennsylvania, which used functional magnetic resonance imaging (fMRI) technology to scan the brains of respondents, found that people who consider themselves to be visual (rather than verbal) learners tended to convert information presented in the form of language into a visual mental representation. The more strongly an individual identified as being a visual learner, the more that individual's visual cortex was activated when reading words. Conversely, those participants who self-identified as verbal learners, upon being shown a picture, displayed brain activity in a region associated with processing sound, suggesting they are converting information received as an image into a form of language (Thompson-Schill, Kraemer and Rosenberg, 2009). It is likely that future research will provide added insights.

In the meantime, thinking about how you learn best as an individual, recognising your preferred learning styles, and carrying out activities to strengthen other styles, can help you to become a more effective student. For example, if you are an activist, tending to jump in with both feet first, you could consider spending some time reflecting on previous experiences and identifying relevant theories before taking action.

Memory techniques

Memory is the ability to store and recall information. All learning, regardless of learning style, is based on memory. Many things conjure up memories: sounds, sights, scents, touch, tastes, emotional feelings and physical movement. The more senses that are actively involved in an experience, the more likely it is to be remembered clearly. In addition to multi-sensory experiences, people generally remember things that are:

- of particular interest
- first and last in a sequence
- concrete, rather than abstract
- linked or associated with something familiar
- absurd, comical, vulgar, rude, or bizarre
- in picture form
- experienced when in a calm and confident frame of mind

You can use this knowledge to help your memory.

Be, and act, interested

If you are not immediately interested in something, use your acting skills. Lean forward, listen, watch or read actively, as though you are studying the most fascinating subject in the world.

Make sure that you understand

Rephrase material in your own words. Write short notes about it. Make links and associations to other examples, drawing pictures or diagrams.

Revisit your work at least three times; once after approximately 24 hours, again after a week, and again after three or four weeks.

Organisation, association and visualisation techniques

Organisation

This involves activities such as:

- linking things that are visually similar; for example, by colour, or shape, or size

- sequencing, or arranging into a series; for example in alphabetical or date order

- categorising, or putting items into groups with similar characteristics

Example

Max needs to remember a list of 15 successful people with dyslexia for his micro-teach session. He is interested in the reasons for their success and fame, he finds out a little about them, and arranges his list as follows:

Entrepreneurs/business leaders:
Sir Richard Branson
William Hewlett
F. W. Woolworth

Athletes:
Muhammad Ali
Sir Steve Redgrave
Sir Jackie Stewart

Political leaders:
Winston Churchill
Michael Heseltine
John F. Kennedy

Actors:
Orlando Bloom
Keira Knightley
Keanu Reeves

Comedians:
Jay Leno
Robin Williams
Eddie Izzard

(Griggs, 2010)

Now, instead of having a long list of 15 unconnected names to remember, Max has five sets of meaningful categories, with just three names in each.

Association

The more that one item or fact can be associated with others, the better it will be remembered. For example, if you need to remember to take an electrical cable safety cover to a teaching session, think about how and why you are going to use it. Imagine using it, ten times as large as life, to cover a gigantic cable that is writhing across the room like a snake. Having made a clear association between the cable and the safety cover, you are much more likely to remember it.

Visualisation

Picturing a mental image which is connected to the item will help you remember it. Try to apply techniques such as:

- exaggeration – make it much larger than life
- contraction – make it much smaller than it is in reality
- absurdity – make it as nonsensical and bizarre as possible
- colour – use strong, vibrant colours
- movement – animate it
- involve all the senses – try to imagine not only how it looks, but also sounds, smells, tastes and feels

The link system

The link system is useful for memorising notes. Extract a key word from each main point of your notes, and then, thinking of the points carefully, form a vivid mental image for each one, remembering to use the visualisation techniques above. Link or associate the first one to the next, and so on, in turn, until you come to the last one.

Example

Dan is going to deliver his micro-teach on readability. He wants to remember to talk about:

- *white space*
- *leading (the spacing between the lines)*
- *font choice and size*
- *use of upper and lower case*
- *illustrations and overprinting*
- *page layout and page breaks*
- *paper choice*
- *readability*

Example

First, he closes his eyes and creates a vivid and striking image of another planet where all around is bright, dazzling white space.

He then links the next item on his list, leading, to the white space. He visualises aliens on the roof of a building in the white space, stealing lead from a building roof.

He then forgets the white space, and links the aliens taking lead from the building roof to the font, or starting place, on a race track where there are alien horses with wings ready to start a race.

Next he forgets the lead on the roof, and links the font to a huge case with the words 'First Prize' written on it, and a bright ribbon around it.

Dan continues this until the end of his list of eight items. He is then able to remember them all during his micro-teach session.

The story method

In this variation of the link system, the items to be remembered are visualised in the same way, and then woven into a story. It can be more difficult, especially with a longer list, to successfully link all the items together into one flowing and memorable story.

Activity

Think of an occasion when you will need to memorise a list or a series of notes. For example, you may have a list of eight or ten points that you want to make in a presentation, or include in your micro-teach. Use the link system or the story method.

Once you have linked your items, or woven them into a story, cover your list and try to write down the main points in the right order. As you recall the linking words, you should also be able to remember what you wanted to say about each one.

The room system

This memory technique involves identifying a mental image for the item to be remembered, and then linking it to a chosen place or location.

Example

Jenna is attending a PTLLS Award class this evening and has five tasks that she wants to remember to do in readiness: make an entry in her reflective learning journal; print out an assessment task; return a book to the library; get a bottle of water; and get some petrol for her car.

She thinks of her house, and chooses a room that contains as many different objects as possible. Deciding on the kitchen, she takes a slow, mental walk around it. Using all her senses (sight, sound, touch, taste and smell), she takes in all the details of the room and its contents. She then thinks of the tasks to be remembered, in order, linking each task with an individual object in the room, making a vivid mental picture of each as she does so.

When all the tasks to be remembered are linked in her mind to the various objects, she can go through her mental walk around the kitchen, recalling the tasks she has placed along the way.

1. *Object: Kitchen table*
   Task: Reflective learning journal (RLJ) entry
   Image: Kitchen table with a giant RLJ as a tablecloth.

Continued

2. *Object:*   *Microwave*
   Task: *Printing assessment*
   Image: *Printed paper pouring out of the microwave.*

3. *Object:*   *Washing machine*
   Task: *Return book to the library*
   Image: *A bright red book spinning in the washer/drier.*

4. *Object:*   *Kitchen sink*
   Task: *Get a bottle of water*
   Image: *Bottles of water popping out of the taps.*

5. *Object:*   *Refrigerator*
   Task: *Buy petrol*
   Image: *The refrigerator in the shape of a petrol can.*

Using the techniques in this chapter will help you become a more effective student which should help towards successful achievement of your PTLLS Award.

Summary

In this chapter you have learned about:

- meeting the Lifelong Learning professional teaching standards

- interpreting the skills needed for the PTLLS Award

- becoming an expert learner

Theory focus

Books

Fleming, N. (2005) *Teaching and learning styles: VARK strategies.* Honolulu: Honolulu Community College.

Gardner, H. (1983) *Frames of mind.* New York: Basic Books.

Gravells, A. (2012a) *Preparing to Teach in the Lifelong Learning Sector,* (5th Edn.) London: Learning Matters.

Gravells, A. (2012b) *Passing PTLLS Assessments,* (2nd Edn.) London: Learning Matters.

Honey, P. and Mumford, A. (1992) *The manual of learning styles,* (3rd Edn.) Maidenhead: Peter Honey Associates.

Websites

Coffield, F., Moseley, D., Hall, E. and Ecclestone, K. (2004). *Learning styles and pedagogy in post-16 learning: A systematic and critical review* [online] available at https://crm.lsnlearning.org.uk/user/order.aspx?code=041543 (accessed 28/01/2012).

Griggs, K. (2010) *Famous celebrity x's* [online] available at www.xtraordinary people.com/celebrity

Institute for Learning – www.ifl.ac.uk

Learning Styles:

BBC/Open University (2004) *Learning Styles* [online] available at www.open2. net/survey/learningstyles

Fleming, N. (2009) *VARK – A Guide to Learning Styles* [online] available at www. vark-learn.com/english/page.asp? p=questionnaire

Gardner, H. *'Multiple Intelligences'* (date unknown) from *The Distance Learning Technology Resource Guide, by Carla Lane* (Howard Gardner) [online] available at www.tecweb.org/styles/gardner.html

Honey and Mumford (1992) – *Learning styles* (2004) [online] available at www. brainboxx.co.uk/A2_LEARNSTYLES/ pages/learningstyles.htm

Thomson-Shill, S., Kraemer, D. and Rosenberg L. (2009) PHILADELPHIA [online] available at www.upenn.edu/pennnews/news/visual-learners-convert-words-pictures-brain-and-vice-versa-says-penn-psychology-study (accessed 28/01/2012).

(VAK) Discover your preferred learning style (2004) [online] available at www. brain-boxx.co.uk/A3_ASPECTS/pages/VAL_quest.htm

LLUK (2007a) *Further Education Workforce Reforms* [online] available at http:// webarchive.nationalarchives.gov.uk/20090410034712/lluk.org/3272.htm

LLUK (2007b) *Professional Standards* [online] available at www.education.gov. uk/publications/standard/publicationDetail/Page1/LLUK-00559-2007

Skills Funding Agency (2011) *The Qualifications and Credit Framework (QCF)* [online] available at http://qcf.skillsfundingagency.bis.gov.uk/

Introduction

In this chapter you will learn about:

- getting the most from taught sessions
- effective note-taking
- keeping notes and information safely
- making the most of group activities

There are activities and examples to help you reflect on the above which will assist your understanding of getting the best out of taught sessions.

Getting the most from taught sessions

Taught sessions are those sessions where you receive information from your PTLLS teacher. This could be as part of a group, a one-to-one session or even electronically. As well as the time attending taught sessions, the PTLLS Award has around 72 hours allocated for self-study. During this time, you will be able to carry out independent self-directed learning and research to help you to complete your assessments and to find out more about the areas that you find especially interesting or relevant.

Taught sessions may take place face-to-face as part of a group and may be held in a conventional classroom, community hall, room at work, or any other relevant setting. They may be spread over a number of weeks, or compressed into an intensive programme over a few days, either consecutively or as part of a day release programme. Learning could also be undertaken using a blended approach: partly face-to-face in a classroom and partly through distance or online delivery, using a virtual learning environment (VLE) such as Moodle, Blackboard, Wimba or Bodington. Using a VLE, the teacher can upload the learning resources for the online sessions via the internet, so that students are able to access them from any computer with an internet connection. Students and teachers are also able to communicate through discussion forums. In this way, learning can be supported 24 hours a day, seven days a week. You may even attend your taught sessions in a learning environment within a three-dimensional online world such as Second Life. If you have enrolled on a distance learning or online programme, where all the taught content is delivered electronically, you will study from home or another suitable environment such as an office, library or a cyber cafe and may meet other members of your programme only virtually, or even not at all. If you are currently teaching, you will need a mentor, someone in the same specialist subject area as your own, who can give you help and support as you progress.

No matter how you are studying for the PTLLS Award, or where your learning for the taught sessions takes place, it is important for you to prepare and organise yourself so that you can get the best out of this time.

In order to get the most from your PTLLS Award taught sessions, you need to think about how you learn best. Consider how you have approached different taught sessions in the past. Think about what worked well that you could re-use, and what you might need to change, and how. Make sure you are comfortable when you set out to learn: that you have had enough to eat; are dressed for comfort; and have all the tools you need around you, including spectacles (if worn), paper, pens and highlighters. Try to make sure that you leave any worries outside the learning environment and, if possible, arrive early so that you are not rushing. Allow yourself time to get to know the other students on your PTLLS Award programme as you will also learn from their knowledge and experience.

You have needs as a student, in exactly the same way that your students will. Sometimes when struggling to keep up with work, personal commitments and study, it is easy to forget to meet personal learning needs.

Activity

Think about a programme of study you have followed in the past that was successful. Make a list of the things that you think contributed to this. Why was this and can you use these tactics to help you now?

Thinking back, in the list of things that contributed to a successful learning experience, you probably noted that the venue was accessible and comfortable, with adequate heating, good lighting and ventilation. There was, most likely, a good group dynamic where group members and teacher were respectful and supportive of each other in a safe environment. You were probably highly motivated to learn a subject, which you recognised was important and useful, and you probably experienced a real sense of achieving your goal.

Sometimes, if a subject seems interesting or relevant, or a goal is particularly important, feelings of loneliness or hunger might go unnoticed. When progress is not so good, however, attention might turn to 'comfort snacks'. Make sure that, for such times, there are some healthy, energy-providing food and drinks in the cupboard or fridge, or in your study bag.

Activity

Look at the following checklist to help you to get the best out of any learning environment. Tick the aspects that apply and consider what else you may need to do before attending your next taught session.

Do I always arrive on time for my sessions?	Whenever possible arrive on time or a little early for teaching sessions. This not only enables an organised and relaxed start to the session, but is considerate of others. It also allows time to get to know other students.	☐
Do I always make sure I have enough to eat?	As adults, with busy lives, skipping meals often seems inevitable. Thinking ahead and planning meals and/or snacks can lead to an improvement in your comfort and your learning.	☐
Do I always make sure I have a bottle of water?	Keep drinking water with you (preferably in a sports bottle to prevent spillage). Most people need between six and eight glasses of water every day to: • regulate body temperature • help the body to absorb nutrients • convert food into energy Moderate dehydration can cause headaches and dizziness, and thirst can cause memory, attention and concentration to decrease by about 10 per cent.	☐

Do I always remember all accessories and equipment?	Remember to take any accessories or equipment you need to be able to participate fully in the programme; for example, spectacles, pen and paper for note-taking, any coloured overlays needed for reading, etc.	☐
Do I make sure my teacher is aware of any specific needs I have?	Ensure that your teacher is aware of any specific needs that you might have, and that these can be met; for example handouts in a large font, on a coloured background, or available electronically.	☐
Do I try to attend every session if I possibly can? If I can't attend, for any reason, have I made study-buddy arrangements?	It is always difficult to catch up effectively with the content of missed sessions. Make sure that you have all the dates and times of your taught sessions displayed clearly in a prominent place, and keep a note of your study buddy's contact details somewhere easy to find, just in case.	☐

Study buddies

Although it is important to attend all the taught sessions of a programme so that you don't miss anything, sometimes it is not always possible. It is a good idea, on the first session of your attendance to find a study buddy. Study buddying is a two-way arrangement where, if you have to be away during part of or the whole of a session, your study buddy will collect handouts for you and create an extra copy of their session notes, which they will write with a little extra care because they know you are going to have to read them. If you can also arrange to meet up for half an hour or so before the next session, for a handover, so much the better. Study buddying makes it much easier to catch up on any missed material, and it can be enjoyable and productive spending a few minutes reviewing and catching up if time permits. It is also useful to keep in touch with them between sessions, perhaps discussing reading and research findings.

Activity

Consider a learning experience that was not so productive. What reasons can you identify for this and why did this happen?

In the less-productive learning situation, was perhaps the room too hot or too cold? Were you hungry or thirsty during sessions, with no facilities available on site to access refreshments? Maybe there was minimal group interaction, and/or a lack of feedback or support from your teacher?

Learning goals

It's important to have goals to work towards, to ensure you keep on track with your assessments. You will probably discuss these with your teacher early on in the programme. When you are identifying these, you might want to look more widely than developing your skills, knowledge and understanding of teaching. For example, you might want to develop some aspects of information communication technology (ICT) such as learning how to produce a computer-generated presentation, or you might want to acquire skills and techniques that help you overcome nerves when presenting to a group.

Activity

Look at the checklist below. Is there anything on the list that you would like to include as a personal goal for development? What about anything that is not on the list, but that you might like to add? There are some blank spaces at the end for you to include your own ideas.

By the end of the PTLLS Award programme, I want to be able to:	
Gain the qualification.	☐
Decide whether teaching is for me.	☐
Develop the skills of an inspirational teacher.	☐
Use a range of different teaching and learning methods.	☐
Use different strategies to motivate students.	☐
Manage and promote equality and diversity in the classroom.	☐
Plan a scheme of work.	☐
Write effective session plans.	☐
Assess students effectively.	☐
Meet challenges with greater self-confidence.	☐

Use my own preferred learning styles effectively to improve the way I learn.	☐
Improve grammar, spelling and/or punctuation.	☐
Overcome nerves when presenting to a group.	☐
Critically and objectively reflect on, and revise, my own teaching practice.	☐
Give feedback appropriately and confidently.	☐
Receive and use feedback from others in a constructive way.	☐
Develop my ICT skills – word processing, presentations, spreadsheets, other.	☐
Improve my confidence.	☐
	☐
	☐
	☐

During your learning, take time to re-visit your personal goals regularly, noting your achievements and also areas where you might need to refocus. You might decide to allow yourself a small treat for each goal achieved to help your motivation. Remember that the PTLLS Award could change your life, both as a teacher and as a student, if you identify and focus clearly on what you want to get out of it.

Example

Sally is following a PTLLS Award programme held in her local village hall; an old draughty building, with one teaching room that has an erratic heating system dependent upon a coin meter, and no social facilities. The teacher knows her subject inside out, and is enthusiastic, but provides little feedback to her group of 12 students.

Sally determines to get the best she can out of this learning situation by:

- *preparing a pre-packed snack, including a flask of hot soup, for the break mid-session*

- *making a point of arriving early for the session so that she can settle in comfortably and exchange views and ideas with some of the other students*

- *taking a bottle of drinking water*

Continued

- *wearing several layers of clothing, so that she can easily and quickly adapt to the changing ambient temperature*

- *setting her own personal short-term goals and self-assessing her achievement, allowing herself a small reward for each goal achieved*

- *making notes of points on which she specifically wants the teacher's feedback, so that she remembers to ask*

- *keeping a reflective learning journal showing her progress towards her personal goals*

Effective note-taking

Whatever system you use for note-taking, make sure that you always use one size of paper. This helps with easy filing and retrieval of your notes. A4 is generally a good choice (30 cm x 21 cm): it is available in a range of colours, with and without lines, fits into standard folders or binders, and is easy to manage. When note-taking, always leave a wide margin on the right-hand side to make additional notes and comments, and to follow up references and research. When hand-writing notes, be careful to write the date on each page, and number each page in order as you write it. If you are using a computer to make your notes, set up a footer (see Chapter 6) to automatically include this information at the bottom of each page. In this way, if your notes should happen to become mixed up later on, they are much easier to locate and re-file. If you are filing your notes using a session-by-session system, it is also helpful to make a note of the date on any printed learning materials you are given.

Activity

Think back to a time when you took notes from a learning session or a meeting. What were the positive and negative aspects:

- *during the note-taking process itself?*

- *afterwards when you reviewed the material?*

Often, note-taking can be a fraught activity. Frantic efforts to keep up result in feelings of frustration during the note-taking process itself, with much of the information being missed, and afterwards what is left can be illegible, unclear and without meaning.

It is important to make sure, when taking notes during a taught session, that you:

- continue to engage fully with the session, entering into any discussions
- identify and make sense of the key points
- capture enough detail for your notes to be meaningful and make sense

Any attempt to write down exactly what is said or written is likely to result in a failure on all counts. Writing down key words or phrases, or making notes by missing out the vowels in words, will help speed up your writing.

After the session, it is important to review your notes as soon as possible, annotating and clarifying any unclear sections while the content is still fresh in your memory. When you come to revisit your notes, it is important that they provide enough detail to:

- revise and recall the material covered, for use in your assessments
- direct you to further reading and research
- enable you to accurately reference other authors' material

Note-taking is an active form of learning: you actively engage with material that you would otherwise receive in a passive form through listening or reading; and by choosing the right note-taking methods and techniques you can transform your notes into a form that really suits the way you think and learn.

Activity

On a piece of A4 paper, note down at least five reasons why you might make notes during your PTLLS Award programme.

How many of the following reasons did you come up with?

1. Note-taking is an active process, which helps you to remember the content (even more so if you have strong kinaesthetic learning preferences).

2. Taking notes helps you to concentrate on the material you are learning.

3. Notes can be useful in comparing and contrasting different theories, principles and ideas.

4. Notes can be used to revisit key facts and theories quickly.

5. Putting notes into your own words can help you to understand difficult concepts.

6. Notes offer opportunities to revisit and revise material to aid learning.

7. Notes can make a large amount of information much more manageable.

8. You can personalise your notes to make them more memorable to you.

9. Notes are useful when planning and writing assessments and for later reference in a work situation.

10. Notes enable you to discuss your work with others; for example, your study buddy or peers.

Some tips for effective note-taking

- Be selective with your note-taking; make notes of the main facts only, not examples or anecdotes.

- When note-taking from a lecture or discussion, use the structure to work out what is important. Words or phrases such as 'a key point is...' or 'the main impact of this...' are important indicators, as is information being repeated, and the use of pauses for emphasis.

- When note-taking from written material, make use of features in the text itself, such as headings and sub-headings, emboldened text, larger font size, underlining, etc., to determine the key points.

- Listen, or read, actively, staying engaged with the material throughout the session, and pace your note-taking.

- Use symbols, abbreviations and keywords to reduce the amount you need to write. Some short forms already exist, such as + or & (and), = (equals), @ (at), e.g. (for example), and i.e. (that is). You can make up others for frequently occurring words or phrases; perhaps using 4 for 'for', S for 'student', T for 'teacher', or 'SoW' for 'Scheme of Work'. Long words can often be shortened, without losing meaning; for example, assessment can be effectively reduced to 'assmt'. (It can also be a useful trick to use a short form for longer words or phrases when word processing your assessments, and then complete them in full by using the global search and replace facility (see Chapter 6).)

- Use colours to identify different themes, styles or approaches. Make sure you have a set of highlighters or coloured pens with you.

- Review your notes as soon as possible after you have written them, and add any necessary clarification or expansion. This has two main benefits.

1. You will be able to make sense of your notes much more easily while the session is still fresh in your mind.
2. Reviewing learning helps transfer into long-term memory.

- Leave out words such as: *a, an, the, is, are, was, were, of,* and pronouns such as: *(s)he, it(s), this, that, these, those, them.* Be careful, however, not to leave out any words essential to meaning.

- Ignore spelling, punctuation and grammar when note-taking, unless the correct form is essential to meaning.

- If you are taking direct quotations from other people's work, remember to enclose them in speech marks and include the full reference straight away. If you are working at level 4, you will need to include quotations and citations (where you paraphrase another author's work) in your assessments. Making a table on the last page of your assessment, or keeping a separate document, where you enter reference details as you go along, is a good way of making sure all your sources are acknowledged. For example, the entry for this book would be as follows.

Surname	Initials	Date	Title	Place of Publication	Publisher
Williams,	J. K.	(2012)	*Study skills for PTLLS (2nd edn)*	London	Learning Matters

For further details about Harvard referencing, see Chapter 5.

Example

Aliya has taken notes from a workshop regarding schemes of work. She has used some of the tips to help her.

SoW – essential 4 groups. Do in advance.
Must include:
Overall:

- *Who for*
- *Subject*
- *Content*
- *Ordering, sequencing*
- *Sessn lengths/times, room*

Example

- *Each sessn:*
- *Aims & objs or LO*
- *Key topics*
- *T activity*
- *S -"-*
- *Assmt*
- *Resources*
- *E&D, sustainability, ECM, func skills*

Sometimes you can highlight or underline material to draw out the key points on printed learning materials you are given, avoiding the need to create your own notes. You might also be happy to annotate textbooks, making comments and critical observations in the margins, whereas other students will prefer to keep their books in original condition. Do not, however, make notes within books borrowed from libraries or other people.

Different types of note-taking

When you do have to create your own notes, the two main ways in which this can be done are:

1. by taking traditional linear, sequential, notes;
2. by taking nuclear or pattern notes, which can be added to in any order.

You can use various forms of these, depending upon your context, the final purpose of the notes, and your preferred learning style.

Linear note-taking

Linear note-taking (where notes are entered sequentially in order, as lines of text) is probably the most frequently-used note-taking method. This form of note-taking can be useful for analytical tasks where you separate a topic into its main parts or important features and consider their relationship to one another. Linear notes often follow a structure that is developed through sections and sub-sections, using increasing levels of indentation on the page. Ideas and information are classified together in hierarchies or sets, using only key words (see Figure 2.1).

Example

Zach has taken some linear notes during a session on learning styles. He has structured his notes in the order they were delivered in the session, leaving spaces between the headings so that he can go back and add any further details needed.

Note the wide right-hand margin to add further detail later.

Learning styles	*21 June 2012 – page 1*

<u>Types</u>

- Honey and Mumford
  - Activist
  - Pragmatist
  - Reflector
  - Theorist

- VARK
  - Visual
  - Aural
  - Read-Write
  - Kinaesthetic

- Howard Gardner
  1) Verbal/linguistic
  2) Mathematical/logical
  3) Musical
  4) Inter-personal
  5) Intra-personal
  6) Visual-spatial
  7) Bodily kinaesthetic
  8) Naturalist

Implications for teaching

- Mix of T&S methods
- Resources
- Group dynamics
- Student response time

Figure 2.1 Linear notes

Nuclear or pattern note-taking

Many people prefer to take notes in a nuclear or non-linear way, working outwards from the centre. Spray diagrams, mind maps, spider diagrams and concept maps are all examples of nuclear or pattern note-taking, in which ideas or information can be presented through drawings and diagrams. Making notes in this way can help you to think more imaginatively, especially if you have a strong visual preference, i.e. prefer to learn by seeing. The visual representation, with the use of colour, pictures, drawings, symbols and arrows, can help to convey meaning by showing the relationship between concepts, and highlighting important points. Pattern or nuclear notes have the added advantage that information can be entered in any sequence, unlike linear notes for which there needs to be some structure in place from the outset.

Spray or spider diagrams are ideal note-taking instruments as they can be used to summarise other people's ideas. Mind maps and concept maps are useful for developing your own ideas on a subject; for example, to sort ideas after brainstorming sessions and to organise information when planning a report or assessment.

Figure 2.2 shows a spray diagram about ground rules. A spray diagram involves quickly jotting down all your ideas on a subject and then linking them up to make connections.

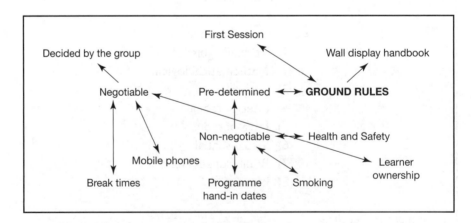

Figure 2.2 A spray diagram about ground rules

In a spider diagram, or concept map, the core topic is shown in the image or circle in the centre of the diagram. Main themes are linked by branches from this core. Some of these themes then have sub-themes that branch outwards from the main branches. The points closer to the centre are usually more general, with points to the outside of the diagram becoming more detailed and specific.

It can be really satisfying to draw a spider diagram or concept map. The best way to approach it is as follows.

1. Use a sheet of plain paper (A4 or larger). Using pre-lined paper can restrict the free flow of ideas;

2. Position the paper in landscape view, with the long edge at the top. This gives more space from left-to-right (as you write).

3. Use brightly coloured crayons or pens, draw an image or symbol that represents your core topic in the centre of the paper. This should be no more than 2" or 5cm high or wide.

4. Label this core image clearly.

5. Use different colours, draw main branches off the core image. Make the branches thicker near the core, and let them start to thin out towards the ends.

6. Label each of the ideas coming out from the core, using just one word, taking up the length of the branch.

7. Develop new ideas, shown by smaller branches coming out from each main branch, drawing pictures or symbols for each if you wish.

8. Remember to have fun with your creation. Use colour and dimension imaginatively. Exaggerate. Add a little humour and absurdity. Make visual associations to other relevant concepts and memories.

Drafting initial thoughts on sticky notes and then moving them around until you are happy with their final positioning can be an effective way to start a mind map or concept map, and works particularly well if you are mapping as part of a group exercise. In this way, the different concepts can be moved around, re-positioned and categorised several times until they reach optimum position. Refer to Buzan World at www.buzanworld.com/Mind_Maps.htm for examples of spider diagrams and mind maps.

Other note-taking resources

Remember that handwritten notes are not the only source of useful information. If you have a mobile phone with a camera, or a small digital camera, you can take photographs of some of the flipchart pages and graphic organisers resulting from group work. Using tape or digital voice recorders can also be a useful addition to your own note-taking; but do remember to ask first if everyone is happy for you to do this during the taught sessions. Sharing notes with peers is another way of enhancing the information that can be taken from a taught session. Any of these methods can be a useful addition to your own note-taking, but should never be used as an alternative, unless of course, you are unable to attend a session, in which case your study buddy can create a set of notes for you.

When you have taken your notes, you might like to make a 'Wordle' from them (see Figure 2.3, which shows a 'Wordle' of this chapter) and use this to remind you of the key points of the session. A wordle is like a doodle but contains key words to help you remember topics.

Figure 2.3 Wordle created from the contents of Chapter 2 using www.wordle.net

Keeping notes and information safely

You might receive a large amount of information while you are working towards the PTLLS Award. You will need to develop an effective filing system for:

- printed learning materials given to you by your teacher

- notes you take during the taught sessions

- notes you take during paired and group discussions and activities with your peers

- notes made from your own reading and research

- hard copies of other relevant materials

Whichever way you decide to store your notes, it is important that you start your study with an appropriate filing system which is organised and to hand. Your system should enable you to divide your notes into easy-to-find categories or sections. Possibly the easiest way to store your notes is in a lever arch file, so that papers can be easily inserted, removed, and refiled or repositioned as necessary. Whatever your choice of container, you should include dividers to mark the partitions you have chosen, possibly:

- in date order, session-by-session

- by assessment topic

- divided into the four units or the 12 learning outcomes of the PTLLS Award:

Roles, responsibilities and relationships in lifelong learning

1. Understand own role and responsibilities in lifelong learning.
2. Understand the relationships between teachers and other professionals in lifelong learning.
3. Understand own responsibility for maintaining a safe and supportive learning environment.

Understanding inclusive learning and teaching in lifelong learning

1. Understand learning and teaching strategies in lifelong learning.
2. Understand how to create inclusive learning and teaching in lifelong learning.
3. Understand ways [how]* to create a motivating learning environment.

Using inclusive learning and teaching approaches in lifelong learning

1. Be able to plan inclusive learning and teaching sessions.
2. Be able to deliver inclusive learning and teaching sessions.
3. Be able to evaluate own practice in delivering inclusive learning and teaching.

Principles of assessment in lifelong learning

1. Understand [how]* types and methods of assessment [are]* used in lifelong learning.
2. Understand ways [how]* to involve learners in the assessment process.
3. Understand requirements for keeping records of assessment in lifelong learning.

Note: * denotes very slight alternative wording for level 4

Activity

Think about how you want to store and retrieve your notes and materials. Do you want to be able to find them session-by-session, by assessment topic, by unit or by each PTLLS Award learning outcome? What resources will you need to do this quickly and effectively?

Once you have acquired a suitable container and dividers, and decided on the structure of your file, you will need to ensure that it is quick and easy to keep up to date. Using note paper that is pre-punched to suit your folder will save time. You will be able to file your handwritten notes from sessions straight away, so that they are easy to find when you next need to refer to them. Taking along a small hole-punch to the sessions will mean you can file away printed learning materials as they are issued. Alternatively, you could invest in some A4 hole-punched plastic pockets, although if you do use these, make sure that all your notes can be seen without the need to remove pages from the pockets. Accidentally slipping a page of notes behind or between other notes in a plastic pocket is one of the easiest ways to guarantee hours of frustrated searching.

Remember that, as well as a file for your own notes and materials, you will need a file for your portfolio of evidence which will be submitted for formal assessment. The latter should only contain evidence of work produced to meet the PTLLS Award assessment criteria, and might be a paper copy or an electronic version.

Making the most of group activities

The PTLLS Award is designed to meet the needs of students who are not yet teaching (pre-service) and those who are practising teachers (in-service), across a wide range of subjects in a variety of teaching contexts and environments. The following are some examples of these.

Teaching contexts	Environments
Adult and community learning …	Community halls and schools
Further education …	Colleges on campus sites
Offender learning …	Prisons, probation centres
Third sector, for example: …	Community centres and family centres
● voluntary and community organisations	Learning buses or lorries
● charities	
● social enterprises	
● co-operatives	
● mutuals	
● housing associations, etc.	
Work-based learning …	Various places of employment

If you are in a group where there is the opportunity to collaborate with others, taking advantage of this will help you to learn from your peers as well as your teacher. You can find out about various responsibilities, challenges, strategies and conditions in different organisations. You might also find it helpful to discuss and swap resources and learning materials.

Activity

Think about your strengths and teaching and learning experiences to date. Write a list of five key areas of skills, knowledge or understanding you could share with other group members. Consider your unique talents and abilities. What is it that you do especially well and enjoy doing that can be difficult for other people? How could you pass your skills on to others?

When you are working with others in your PTLLS Award group, remember to take notice of how they address different situations and challenges. You can then adopt any strategies you see that work, and avoid or adapt those that do not.

Having identified your key strengths, also think about two or three key areas that you would like to improve. How could you learn from others to help yourself?

The benefits of learning in groups are far wider than simply offering the potential to transfer skills, and knowledge. Consider the TEAM perspective:

Together
Everyone
Achieves
More.

Research has shown that co-operative groups perform better than independent individuals (Laughlin and Ellis, 1986). When working as a team, the results achieved are greater than the sum of the individual parts in terms of:

- quality of decisions

- better judgements

- motivation

- speed of learning

- support

This does not happen straight away, though, and it will take time for you to feel comfortable working in group situations.

Group development

Groups take time to form. Initially all the group members may be apprehensive about the programme and its demands, and uncertain about discussing hopes and concerns with others, whether face-to-face or through the use of discussion forums in a blended or online programme. As the programme gets underway, however, everyone will start to find out more about each other. Icebreaker exercises are a good way to get to know others in the early stages of a programme and it is a good idea to play an active part in these, even if you do not normally enjoy them. Whether conducted face-to-face or online through discussion forums, etc., they are an opportunity to forge new friendships and develop new skills.

Soon the group should start to settle and effective group working will become the norm. Many contacts and friendships sealed during PTLLS Award programmes are maintained beyond, continuing, in some cases, through other programmes, and beyond.

Working effectively with others

Working with others can sometimes prove difficult. The points that follow might help.

1. Remember that each individual has their own beliefs, values and attitudes, to which they are entitled.

2. Recognise and value individual talents and skills.

3. Accept that everyone will be able to contribute positively to the group in some way.

4. Allow all members the opportunity to speak; respect their rights to their views and opinions and remember that their contributions are equally as valuable as your own.

5. Engage fully in all group discussion and activities, remembering not to speak over others.

6. Remember that conflict is natural within a group. Disagreements can highlight and explore different perspectives and approaches.

7. Disagreements should never become personal. If you find yourself challenging something that is said or done, remember to comment on the behaviour and not the person.

Example

During a session on equality and diversity, one of the group members uses the term 'coloured' instead of 'black'. Suneera is upset by this remark, but she is careful to challenge and confront it in a sensitive manner, using a three-step approach.

1. She states the behaviour that has upset her: 'When you refer to black people as coloured ...'

2. She states the impact/effect of the behaviour: 'I feel very upset and hurt,'

3. She goes on to state a preferred future behaviour: 'please use the term "black" in future'.

When working within groups and carrying out joint activities, individuals will usually take up one or more roles and responsibilities. These roles and responsibilities might vary, depending upon the nature and size of the group and the tasks in question. For a group task to be successfully completed, its members will need to effectively share out roles and responsibilities for:

- leading and focusing group members

- ensuring that there is no in-fighting and all members' contributions are valued

- finding creative solutions to problems

- making sure ideas are viable

- acquiring necessary resources

- planning and scheduling tasks

- drawing the overall task to a successful and timely conclusion

- ensuring that everyone in the group is, and feels, involved

Activity

When you next undertake a group activity, note how you approached the different roles and responsibilities outlined. What approaches were taken up by the other group members? What were your own strengths and preferences? Were all of the roles taken up? Was the task effectively completed? This could form the focus of an entry in your reflective learning journal.

A great deal can be learned from observing how your peers approach tasks and situations. Depending upon their learning styles, beliefs, values, attitudes and life experiences, people will react to situations in different ways. When you are next with a group, consider whether you would naturally shy away from an activity and then try to overcome this by getting involved. You might also realise that you tend to take over in certain circumstances when it might be good to sit back and allow others space to develop their own skills.

Much can also be learned from peer evaluation, and from self-evaluation of your own actions and your work. Part of the PTLLS Award will enable you to develop strategies for giving constructive feedback to others, and, equally importantly, experience receiving feedback and acting on it constructively.

Reflecting on the PTLLS Award sessions

Part of the practical assessment for your PTLLS Award involves you demonstrating the qualities of a reflective practitioner. A way of doing this is to look back over each of the PTLLS Award taught sessions that you have attended, preferably soon after the event, and ask yourself some key questions.

- What were the main points I learned?
- How will/could these be useful?
- What else do I want to achieve as a result of this session?
- What did I do? How was I feeling? What was I thinking?
- How did others respond?
- What were the consequences?
- What does this teach me?

- What might I do differently in a similar session in the future, or in my own teaching?

- What impact will it have?

Not only will this reflection contribute towards the entries in your reflective learning journal, but it will also help you to get the best out of your experiences during the taught sessions. For more detailed information on reflective practice and writing reflective learning journals, see Chapter 4.

Summary

In this chapter you have learned about:

- getting the most from taught sessions

- effective note-taking

- keeping notes and information safely

- making the most of group activities

Theory focus

Books

Buzan, T. (1989) *Use your head*, 2nd edn. London: BBC Books.

Gardner, H. (1983) *Frames of mind*. New York: Basic Books.

Gravells, A. (2012a) *Preparing to Teach in the Lifelong Learning Sector,* (5th Edn.) London: Learning Matters.

Gravells, A. (2012b) *Passing PTLLS Assessments,* (2nd Edn.) London: Learning Matters.

Honey, P. and Mumford, A. (1992) *The manual of learning styles,* (3rd Edn.) Maidenhead: Peter Honey Associates.

Laughlin, P. and Ellis, A. (1986). 'Demonstrability and social combination processes on mathematical intellective tasks', *Journal of Experimental Social Psychology,* 22: 177–189.

Websites

Buzan World	www.buzanworld.com/Mind_Maps.htm
Maslow's Hierarchy of Needs	http://maslow.com
Open University (study skills and other modules)	http://openlearn.open.ac.uk
VARK (learning styles)	www.vark-learn.com/english/index.asp
Wordle	www.wordle.net

Introduction

In this chapter you will learn about:

- researching using different media

- choosing and evaluating texts and other resources

- reading texts actively and critically

There are activities and examples to help you reflect on the above which will assist your understanding of how to study for your PTLLS Award.

Researching using different media

Libraries

A good starting place for research can be a library or learning resource centre (LRC). Depending upon where you live, this may be your local library or the library belonging to a college, university or other organisation where you are studying. Take the time to join any local libraries as soon as possible – and obtain a leaflet, or access their website, to gain information such as:

- their opening hours – these might be different in term times and during holidays

- the types of items that are available

- how many items you can borrow at any one time, and for how long

- whether you can reserve books or other media, and, if so, whether this has to be in person, or can be via the telephone or internet

- if there is a fine system for late returns, and, if so, how it works

- if photocopies can be made and, if so, the charges and any restrictions

Activity

If you haven't already joined or visited a library or LRC, make a list of all the products and services you might expect them to provide. Then, take time to visit and join and see what is available that could help with your PTLLS studies.

Some of the more commonly available products and services, besides books that you might find in a library include:

- academic journals and periodicals
- CDs, DVDs and videos
- computers with internet access (often giving free use)
- library services induction from experienced staff
- media reservation service
- newspapers and magazines
- photocopying, laminating and binding equipment or services
- quiet study areas with sockets and space for laptops and other equipment

Finding information in the library

Books

Reference and textbooks are an excellent way of finding out information relating to the subject you are studying. You don't have to read the full book from cover to cover to find what you want; use the index at the back to locate relevant topics and their page number. Books are filed and displayed by subject, broken down into numerical sequence by *call number*, which is shown on the spine of the book. A call number tells you the exact location of the book title in the library, and can be found from the library catalogue which is often electronic. (Detailed information about carrying out electronic searches is included later in this chapter.)

Usual catalogue systems are the Dewey Decimal Classification (DDC), which is the world's most widely used library classification system (OCLC, 2012), or the Library of Congress (LC) system, which is used in many colleges, universities and research libraries. Both systems are now available electronically as well as in hard copy. The DDC system was devised by Melvil Dewey in the 1870s and has been owned by the OCLC (Online Computer Library

Center) since 1988. The 23rd four-volume print edition of the DDC was published in May 2011. This version provides new and updated numbers and topics, as well as tools to improve efficiency, but continues to retain its logical, familiar and easily navigable nature. Because of its user-friendly features, DDC continues to be used in most public and school libraries.

The DDC system is made up of ten main classes or categories between 000 and 900, each divided into ten secondary classes or sub-categories, each having ten subdivisions, as in the following example.

300	is Social Sciences (main category)	
	370	represents Education (sub-category); each sub-category is further sub-divided, e.g. 371 through to 379
		371 school management, special education; 372 primary education; 373 secondary education; 374 adult education; 375 curricula; 376 education of women; 377 schools and religion; 378 higher education; 379 finance, supervision and control of public education.
		Each of these subject areas continues to be further subdivided into smaller and smaller sections, with the call number becoming longer as sections become more specific:
		370.7 represents *Education*, research and related topics;
		370.711 represents teacher training; 370.715 *Continuing Professional Development (CPD)*.

Within the LC system, call numbers can begin with one, two, or three letters, the first letter representing one of the 21 major divisions of the LC system. For example, class L represents education. The second letter, B in the following example, represents a sub-class: Theory and practice of education.

Theory and practice of education:	LB
Together, the sub-class LB2395 denotes *Methods of study in Higher Education*	2395
The decimal indicates filing in decimal order The alpha-numeric reference is usually derived from author's name	M378
The final section of a call number is generally the year of publication	2008

LB2395.M378 2008 is the LC call number for:

Denby, N., Butroyd, R., Swift, H., Price, J. and Glazzard, J. (2008) *Master's level study in education: A guide to success for PGCE students*. Maidenhead: OUP.

It helps to find books if you already know the surname and initials of the writer(s) and the title of the book. If you have only sketchy details, entering the information you do have into the text search field of an online bookstore will often produce the desired results. Once you have this information, be careful to keep it safe and note the date of publication, city or town of publication and publisher's name, for your references list or bibliography. You should also make a note of the call number so that you can find the book again quickly and easily.

Activity

Identify and make a note of the classification system (or systems) used to categorise books in your local library or LRC. Find and look through the shelves of teaching and training books. Look in the index of some of the books to locate relevant topics for your PTLLS assessments; for example, resources. Start a reference log, noting the call numbers of books that you might want to refer to again.

Teaching and learning journals or periodicals

These are useful sources of reference for your assessments because they usually contain the most up-to-date research and developments in teaching. Most journal articles have an abstract at the front which gives you a brief summary of the content. Journals are usually published at regular intervals during the year, and numbered into volumes and issues. Often one volume will contain all the issues, or magazines, published during a calendar year, although issues might be organised into volumes spanning academic years, or other significant time periods. To find a particular journal article, you will need to know the:

- title of the journal, year of publication, and volume number
- name and initials of the author(s)
- title of the article

The above information, together with the issue number and the page numbers, will also be needed for referencing within your work. Again, make sure you keep the referencing details safe, together with any information you extract, and a note of the call number.

Indexes and abstracts

These are separate publications which give a brief overview of journal articles, including who wrote them, where they can be found, and the general idea of the content. Often, you may find that the information from the abstract is sufficient for use in your PTLLS assessment, without needing to read the original article in full. Again, be careful to keep all information safely for referencing.

Electronic information

An increasing amount of information is published electronically and available online. To access an electronic journal or article, you must first access the internet and type the Uniform Resource Locator (URL) or web address into your computer's browser. (A browser is the computer program that makes it possible for you to read information on the internet. Most personal computers use Internet Explorer as standard, while Macs use Safari, although you can choose alternatives such as Firefox, Google Chrome or Opera). A URL is made up of several parts. It is useful to understand these as they can help you gauge the relevance of the information on the website.

As well as accessing information from electronic journals, you can use articles from a variety of different websites. If you do this, you need to be much more careful with your selection, as although there are many useful websites, there are also many published without a review and editing process. Even before you enter a website, there are clues in the URL to help you with this process. A URL is made up of several parts, each of which tells you a little about the site to which it refers. (The table overleaf breaks these down and outlines their meaning.)

When researching, you may know that domain names ending in *.co.uk*, *.com*, *.org*, and *.net* often signify commercial entities whose information may be designed to persuade, rather than to inform. Those ending in *.gov.uk* belong to UK government organisations, whilst those ending in *.ac.uk* or *.sch.uk* are UK academic institutions, and those ending in *.edu* are United States academic institutions. Such sites are likely to include material that lends itself well to the *4As evaluation process* (see page 55). You should, however, always be mindful that you can also find personal webpages of individuals, for example of academics and students, within such sites, and that these might not reflect the institution's views. Usually, these pages are designated by the ~ symbol, for example the URL: http://www.comp. lancs.ac.uk/~dixa which links to the personal pages of Professor Alan Dix at Lancaster University.

Example

Part of address	Meaning
http://	The first part of the web address is the protocol, which tells the web browser the type of server it will be talking to in order to reach the URL. This protocol http:// (short for Hypertext Transfer Protocol), indicates a hypertext document or directory. Remaining parts of the URL do vary depending on the protocol, but most servers use http://
www.	Indicates a page on the world wide web (sometimes www is missing, but where it is included, you can usually leave out http:// and it will insert automatically.
www.ifl.ac.uk	Together, these indicate the web server name, or fully qualified domain name.
ifl.ac.uk	The domain name, in this case, registered to an academic (.ac) organisation in the UK is the part of the name registered for exclusive use (see below for more details).
/iflonline	Finally comes the path through which the web page is retrieved. This part of the address signifies the start of the path indicating a directory or folder on the web server called iflonline and containing a set of related pages within the website.
/joinonline	A sub-folder called joinonline.
/personaldetails.html	A page called personaldetails.html. NB: Most web pages end in .htm, .html or .shtml.
Complete URL: https://www.ifl.ac.uk/iflonline/joinonline/personaldetails.html	

The final part of the *domain name* tells you the type of individual or organisation to whom the website is registered:

Address ending	Description
.co.uk	.co is for companies, and .uk is the country code. For example, www.amazon.co.uk denotes Amazon's UK site.
.com	.com indicates US organisations, but also international ones. (It is the most popular ending.)
.gov.uk	.gov.uk signifies a UK government organisation; for example, the government Department for Education is found at www.education.gov.uk.
ac.uk or .sch.uk .edu	In the UK universities and other educational establishments use .ac.uk while schools use .sch.uk. In the United States, they use .edu for academic institutions. For example, the IfL domain name is www.ifl.ac.uk and that of Harvard University is www.harvard.edu.
.net	This is usually for internet-related organisations or companies.

Activity

Look at the list of useful websites in Appendix 5. Select a couple that you would like to investigate further. Type in the URL for each of the sites and browse or look through the information that is displayed on the screen. If you want to keep a permanent record, or you find it difficult to read from the screen, you can print it out and read it from the hard (paper) copy. It's good to use a highlighter to mark the significant parts you might refer to in your work.

Search engines

Search engines such as Google, www.google.co.uk; Yahoo!, http://uk.yahoo.com; Alta Vista, http://uk.altavista.com; and Ask Jeeves, http://uk.ask.com, search the internet for keywords or phrases, and then display the results, which are unmonitored and unchecked. Searches might deliver huge quantities of information, much of which is out of date, biased, inaccurate, and/or irrelevant, so you need to judge the reliability of all results carefully. Just because someone has published an article on the internet, it does not mean that they have any real knowledge of the subject, or that their writing is impartial. It's also worth remembering that the same article or reference can turn up many times in the search engine results.

When searching you need to be specific with your topic.

- Place the main subject first in your criteria, as some search engines use the first word to establish relevance ranking.
- Structure your search carefully. If you want to:
  - look for all the words that you specify, simply type them into the search field, separated by spaces
  - find an exact phrase, surround it in quotation marks; for example, 'scheme of work'
  - look for any one of the words you specify, type OR in between them; for example, 'session plan' OR 'lesson plan'
  - specify that a word or phrase must appear in any documents listed, put a (+) sign in front it; for example, '+motivation'
  - prevent a word or phrase from appearing, type it into the search field immediately preceded by a hyphen; for example, '-sports'
- Use the keyword *database* in your search: you may find a searchable database on your topic.

- Use more than one keyword, but no more than six to eight.
- Try different spellings; for example, American English, or common mis-spellings.

Example

Afra is researching for her assessment on equality and diversity. Firstly she defines the subject in a sentence.

Promoting equality is an essential role of the teacher in post-16 education.

She goes on to split this sentence into key concepts, discarding everything else: **equality, teacher roles, post-16.**

For each of these, she thinks of synonyms (words with a similar meaning) or related terms that would be useful, including:

- **equality, diversity, inclusion**
- **teacher roles, teacher responsibilities**
- **post-16, post-compulsory, FE, Lifelong Learning**

When entering her search, she uses OR and +:
equality OR diversity OR inclusion +education.

When her first results set comes up, she finds she has a great many references to primary education, so she tries again: **equality OR diversity OR inclusion –primary +education.**

Her results this time are much more worthwhile.

The advanced search option provided by most search engines can also be used to make searches more specific. Instructions vary by search engine, but are generally straightforward to follow, with dedicated boxes often being provided for the functions outlined above. A useful additional feature is that of being able to restrict your search to a particular domain; for example, to just UK sites or to academic or government sites.

A limitation of search engines is that there is a quantity of invisible information that is hidden from them. Some of this more scholarly type information can be found through the search engine Google Scholar: http://scholar.google.co.uk, which searches materials from academic, professional and educational organisations. Because Google Scholar co-operates with publishers to reveal content which is normally inaccessible, it is likely to reveal useful information that is unavailable from the general commercial search engines. Not everything listed on Google Scholar is freely available, however, and you may find yourself unable to open or download certain resources.

Information gateways

One way of helping to ensure that the information you obtain from the internet is current and unbiased, and to cut down on the time you spend searching, is to use academic subject gateways instead of commercial search engines. These subject gateways (also called directories) provide direct links to more academic, reliable information, usually with a brief description of the resource. Maintained by experts in the different subject areas, they have strictly imposed quality criteria and therefore the sites listed on them can be relied on for consistent quality and accurate and trustworthy information. As a result of their focused coverage, you will also probably get a smaller number of 'hits' or results returned, which will save you a great deal of time filtering out those that are unsuitable for your purposes. Subject gateways and online libraries with resources linked to education that you may wish to try include those listed below.

BeCal – Belief, Culture and Learning	A learning gateway which supports citizenship education.	www.becal.net
BUBL Information Service	Aimed at higher education, but useful for further education, you can search by keyword or browse by subject.	www.bubl.ac.uk (not updated since April 2011)*
Eurydice at NFER	Part of the European information network on education.	www.nfer.ac.uk/eurydice
Excellence Gateway (LSIS)	Post-16 learning and skills resources, support and advice, and opportunities to participate and share good practice.	www.excellencegateway. org.uk
IngentaConnect	Access to online journal abstracts and articles, many free of charge.	www.ingentaconnect.com
Intute: Education	A free online service provided by a consortium of seven universities. Access to websites selected and evaluated by subject specialists.	www.intute.ac.uk (not updated since July 2011)*
Pinakes	Links to major subject gateways.	www.hw.ac.uk/libwww/irn/ pinakes/pinakes.html
Questia	A large online library with a broad selection of books and journal articles. There is no charge for searching, but a subscription is required to access publications.	www.questia.com

*Although these sites are no longer being updated, they give access to useful resources provided before that date.

Social bookmarking

Social bookmarking sites are web 2.0 applications (web pages that allow visitors to interact with the web page content). You can use these sites to bookmark useful web pages so that you can record your journey around the world wide web. An advantage of the social bookmarking system, as opposed to bookmarking in a browser, or copying and pasting links into a table in a word processing package, is that because your bookmarks are held centrally, they are available from anywhere at any time, not just from the computer on which you made the bookmark. By giving descriptive tags (keywords) to your bookmarks, you can also make them much easier to manage and organise. Social bookmarking sites can be helpful, not only to keep an online record of web resources that you have found useful, but also to get ideas of other sites to visit, as you will be able to see other sites that are being visited by different people who have tagged some of the same sites as you. It is rather like being able to scan other students' bookshelves for ideas, but on a worldwide scale. Useful bookmarking sites for studying include:

- Citeulike – www.citeulike.org

- Connotea – www.connotea.org

- Delicious – http://delicious.com

- H20 Playlist – http://h2obeta.law.harvard.edu

- LibraryThing – www.librarything.com

- Diigo – www.diigo.com

Activity

If you do not already use social bookmarking, choose and investigate one or two of the sites from the list. Look at the resources behind one or two of the most active tags or take a tour around the website.

If you are impressed, why not register? Remember to keep a note of your registration details.

Choosing and evaluating texts and other resources

Textbooks

When evaluating textbooks to help you study for your PTLLS Award, there is a number of important points to be considered. Referring to the '4As' (Williams, 2010) checking system will help you to spend your study time more effectively by helping you to choose and work from reliable, unbiased sources; or if you do use sources with a bias, accounting for this. The 4As are:

- **A**uthorship and provenance
- **A**spect
- **A**udience and extent
- **A**ccessibility

Authorship

- Does the text seem trustworthy? Who wrote it? What is their reputation?
- How does this text relate to other information on the same subject?
- When was the most recent edition of the book published? When was it last reprinted?

Aspect

- Is there an introduction setting out scope and purpose?
- Are the arguments logical and sound, or is there some dubious reasoning?
- Are the arguments supported by facts and evidence, and fully referenced?
- Are there any alternative explanations to those given by the author?

Audience and extent

- How comprehensive is the information?
- Who are the intended audience (specialists, experts, general public, students, etc.)?

Accessiblity

- Are the level of language and depth and breadth of content accessible, and appropriate for use in your PTLLS assessments?

E-books

It is possible that you are reading this text in an e-book via an e-book reader. Research from 2011 indicated that e-books, and e-book readers, are becoming increasingly popular. Interestingly, their UK popularity seems to be greatest with the older generation. A survey carried out by Silver Poll (www.silverpoll.com) at the start of 2011 found that around 6 per cent of over-55s owned an e-book reader compared to 5 per cent of 18 to 24-year-olds.

An e-book, or *electronic book*, is a book that you can read on screen instead of on paper. E-books are not limited to text; they can include pictures in the same way as conventional books, but also sound clips, animated graphics and video. As well as the potential for multi-media, there are many other advantages of e-books. You can store many book titles effectively in much less physical space than their conventional counterparts; it is now possible to carry a library around with you, offering almost unlimited choice of what to read and research in those spare moments. New titles can be ordered from the comfort of your workspace and delivered to your e-reader instantly. It can be much easier to find the title of the book, and even the text you want, by using the electronic search facility. When using an e-book, you can mark your page with an electronic bookmark and automatically return to it upon re-opening the book. You can also make notes electronically on the text. Some e-books have built-in dictionaries enabling you to click on a word to find out what it means, and reference books often come with extensive collections of references and footnotes.

As well as being able to buy e-books, many are now available to download free of charge or to borrow via an electronic library service. Useful sites to visit include Google Books, the Gutenberg Project, the Hathi Trust and the Open Library. Links to these sites are included at the end of the chapter, and again in Appendix 5 in the Useful Books and Websites section.

E-books are usually read on dedicated e-book readers, also known as e-book devices, or simply e-readers. However, any electronic device that has a text screen display, such as a computer, mobile phone or Personal Digital Assistant (PDA) can act as an e-book reader. Some of the major book retailers have free e-reader applications for PC and Mac desktops as well as iPad, iPhone, Android and Blackberry devices.

Popular dedicated e-book readers include the Amazon Kindle, Barnes & Noble's Nook, WH Smith's Kobo, Pandigital's Novel e-readers and the Sony Reader. The main advantages of dedicated e-book readers are their light and compact nature, better readability especially in bright sunlight, and longer battery life. On the downside, you will have to be connected to a computer with a broadband or wireless link to download texts or manage libraries. Furthermore, e-book readers are limited to the book formats supported by the manufacturers, who often try to lock the reader into only one format. Before investing in an e-reader, it is a good idea to check the format, range and availability of titles through that manufacturer.

The same rules govern the evaluation of e-books as those for conventional books discussed earlier in this chapter.

CD-ROMs and DVD-ROMs

A great deal of educational content is available on pre-recorded CDs and DVDs which are now very cheap to mass produce and purchase. In terms of similarity, CDs and DVDs are both the same size and shape. The use of the affix '–ROM' in this case denotes read-only memory, meaning that data cannot be added or recorded over, it can only be read. Main differences are in the storage, with a CD-ROM having a storage capacity of 650 mega-bytes – roughly equivalent to 6,500 pages, and a DVD-ROM holding over six times the information with a capacity of 4.7 gigabytes. DVDs also access data much more quickly. CDs can be read by both CD and DVD drives, whereas DVDs can be read only by a computer with a DVD drive. The advantages of using CD and DVD discs rather than accessing information via the internet include the absence of connectivity issues and costs, and slow download times. Sound, large graphics, animations and video clips are available with complete user interactivity, and discs can also include outside links to complementary websites. These media should be subjected to simi-lar scrutiny as textbooks and e-books.

Websites

As outlined earlier in this chapter, data on the web can be inaccurate, unre-liable, out of date, and quite possibly biased (showing favouritism to one party or view). Once again, it is useful to use the 4As system as a check (Williams, 2010).

Authorship and provenance

- In the evaluation of information sources, provenance, from the French verb *provenir*, meaning 'to come from', is about origin and authenticity. Does the article or information have a stated author? If so, what is their educational or occupational background? Are they connected with a respected professional association, institution or publisher?

- Is the publisher or website well known in the field, and is it on the recommended reading list?

- Is the website from an official source? The final part of the domain name tells you the type of individual or organisation to whom the website is registered. Official websites such as those belonging to educational or government departments are more likely to be the source of up-to-date and reliable information, not least because they have their reputations to preserve. They usually end in .ac.uk or .gov.uk respectively.

- Does the article itself have a good references list or bibliography with working links to other reputable websites?

- Does the information appear to be accurate? How does it relate to other articles on the same subject?

- When was the information last updated? Is there a date given – for the original publication, and/or for subsequent updates?

- Wikipedia (www.wikipedia.org) contains a wealth of information which is usually presented in a format that is easy to read and absorb. It can often be a good place to start research into a new topic or new terminology. However, unlike traditional encyclopaedias anyone, regardless of their educational or occupational background, can contribute to it. Furthermore, as there is no way to check provenance from the multiple contributors, they cannot be called upon to support their entries. This means that information included in Wikipedia might be inaccurate, biased, or even completely untrue.

If you do decide to use Wikipedia as a starting place for your research, make sure you always:

- use the history and discussion pages linked to an entry to help you decide whether the information merits further investigation

- carry out further investigation by following the references and links provided and finding additional original sources

- satisfy yourself, using the 4As system, that the information is both reasonable to include and able to be accurately acknowledged

- avoid using Wikipedia itself as a reference source in your assignments

Aspect

- From what aspect is the article written? Is there an introductory statement setting out its scope and purpose?

- How objective does the text appear? Is it biased to a particular personal or political viewpoint, and if so, which? Does this matter for your purposes?

- Is the language used informative, or persuasive?

Audience and extent

- How comprehensive is the information?

- What audience does it appear to be aimed at? The type of language used should help you to make an informed judgement here.

Accessiblity

- Do the level of language and depth of study match your needs?

- How accessible is the site and the material on it? Is the site straightforward to navigate? Can you find your way around the information easily?

- Are links to other pages obvious, and working?

- Can you easily print what you need?

Podcasts

The name 'Podcast' originates from 'iPod' and 'broadcast', as originally podcasts were audio programmes formatted to be played on an iPod, although now they can be downloaded to an iPod or an MP3 player. Some are free, and others are sold via the internet. Podcasts can be downloaded or used online (subject to adequate broadband and appropriate software and plug-ins).

Plug-ins are free computer software that let you receive information such as sound, video and animation, so called because they plug in to your browser the first time you download them onto your computer, generally installing automatically. If you visit a site that needs a plug-in, your browser will ask you whether you want to download it. Once installed, you will often have to restart your browser or even your operating system before the plug-in becomes active. Once active however, plug-ins engage automatically whenever they are needed.

Enhanced podcasts (audio podcasts that can display images and sound at the same time) are also now available, and can contain chapter markers, hyperlinks (links to other websites) and artwork. Enhanced podcasting is a very practical way to present information including lectures, slide shows, video clips, etc. Many podcasts are produced by professionals, although, as with website articles, many are also produced by amateurs. Again, the 4As (Williams, 2010) can be used to assess the suitability of podcasts.

Authorship and provenance

- Does the podcast have a stated author? If so, what is their educational or occupational background? Are they connected with a respected professional association, institution or publisher?

- Are sources for further information (websites and email) included in the podcast?

- Does the information appear to be accurate? How does it relate to other information you have found on the same subject?

- When was podcast last updated? Is there a date given – for the original publication, and/or for subsequent updates?

Aspect

- Is there an introduction setting out scope and purpose?

- How objective does the content appear?

- Is effective use made of the presenter, discussions and interviews?

- Is the content biased to a particular personal or political viewpoint, and if so, which – and does it matter?

- Is the language used informative, or persuasive?

Audience and extent

- How comprehensive is the information?

- What audience does it appear to be aimed at? Again, the type of language used should help you to make an informed judgement here.

Accessibility

- Do the level of language and depth of study match your own specific needs?

- Is the topic well structured and organised and presented in an interesting and imaginative way?

- Are vocals clear without background noise or popping, with the presenters able to be clearly heard above background music and effects?

- Are any audio effects used constructively to enhance the listening and learning experience?

Carefully-chosen podcasts can be an excellent source of information and learning. Audio podcasts have the advantage that they can be downloaded and listened to conveniently during time that might otherwise be downtime, such as when travelling on a train or a bus, or when walking or exercising.

Virtual learning environment (VLE) learning tools

Your PTLLS Award may be supported to a greater or lesser extent by the use of a virtual learning environment (VLE) such as Moodle, Blackboard, WebCT or Bodington (see Chapter 2). VLEs can be accessed from any computer with an internet connection, providing a flexible learning environment. If the timetable, activities and related materials are available on a VLE from the beginning of your studies, you can use this information to organise work, family commitments and plan time for studying. Using a VLE as part of a distance or blended learning programme can substantially reduce time and expenses travelling to and from classes. A VLE can provide opportunities for study at convenient times outside face-to-face sessions. If you find yourself unable to attend a session, and the learning materials are available via a VLE, you will be able to access them (subject to computer and internet access) and read through them before the next session, which will enable you to clarify anything that was unclear. Another big advantage of VLEs is that you can receive immediate feedback from simulations and quizzes, rather than having to wait for homework to be marked. Also, if you know that the all learning materials are available on the VLE, it makes it easier to listen, ask questions and engage fully in the face-to-face activities, without having to worry about taking detailed notes as you can access the information later.

Reading texts actively and critically

Skimming

It is useful to skim texts (and other materials) to get a general idea of their content and usefulness. Skimming involves looking over a piece of information quickly to obtain its gist, purpose and tone. When skimming, you do not read the whole text word for word. If, as a result of skimming, you find that the content appears useful, you can allocate more time to examine it in detail. When skimming, use as many clues as possible to give you background information.

- Read the title and sub-headings.

- Note comments made in the introduction, abstract and summary.

- Identify the author(s).

- Establish when the text was written.

- Look at illustrations to predict the contents.

- Read the first and last sentences of each paragraph, which should introduce and conclude the topic or idea respectively.

Activity

Next time you visit the library, look at a textbook that you think might be helpful in your PTLLS studies and skim through it to establish its general idea, purpose and tone. Once you have done this, if the book appears promising, remember to make notes of the content, reference details and the call number so that you are able to use the information you have extracted, and find the book again quickly on a subsequent visit.

Scanning

Scanning has a different purpose, this time looking, not for the gist, but for detail. Texts are scanned for two purposes. The first is to glean specific information; for example, a name, or date, a particular reference or information. Once this information is found, the text can be disregarded without further investigation. The second purpose for scanning is to rapidly explore a text to see if it warrants skimming before more detailed inspection. You might, for example, scan for a keyword or heading. When searching through electronic texts, it is useful to identify two or three keywords that might supply the information you are looking for, and then enter these, one by one, into the find or search facility. In this way you can quickly see whether the text in question is likely to have the content you require.

Example

Ibrahim wants to quickly check out a website he has found on the internet that looks as though it might provide some useful information for his assessment task regarding embedding functional skills.

He decides on six key terms, which are:

- *functional skills*
- *literacy*
- *numeracy*
- *ICT*
- *English*
- *maths*

He quickly carries out an automatic search for each of these, noting the number of hits he gets.

His scanning exercise delivers only three hits, all for ICT, so he discards it as a potential reference source.

Previewing

Previewing a text is using as much advance information about it as possible to decide its contents and context. You can do this by looking through:

- the blurb, a short promotional description, usually on the back page
- the abstract, if there is one
- the index
- contents pages
- references list
- bibliography
- titles
- headlines
- illustrations

This should give you a strong impression of the text, making subsequent detailed reading much more straightforward.

Active reading

When you are reading a document in detail, it can help to highlight, under-line and annotate as you read. This stimulates visual and kinaesthetic pathways, and emphasises the information which you could review again later. It also helps to stop your mind wandering, keeping it focused on the material. If you are using an electronic source, or do not wish to mark the hard copy, it may be worth printing or photocopying the information first.

When reading difficult material with new terminology, photocopy or compile a glossary, keeping it beside you as you read. Note down the key concepts in your own words to help your understanding.

SQ3R reading technique

Rowntree (1998) suggests the *SQ3R* (**S**urvey, **Q**uestion, **R**ead, **R**ecall and **R**eview) approach to effective reading and note-taking.

1. Survey the chapter or book, leafing through to note the layout, look-ing at first and last chapters or first and last lines of paragraphs, and the headings used, examining any diagrams, charts or pictures, familiaris-ing yourself with the reading. (This is similar to the stage of previewing outlined above.)

2. Question yourself about the structure of the text, thinking about the questions you will need to keep in mind while reading. Ask yourself how current the material is and how relevant it is to your own purposes.

3. Read actively, and quickly, looking to identify the main points of the text.

4. Recall the main points of the text, writing them down, together with any important facts and opinions that help support them. (Remember to note necessary reference information.)

5. Review, repeating stages 1–3, making sure that you have not over-looked anything, amending your notes, if necessary. Read through your notes once more to check them, and identify where the information fits into your assessment.

Activity

Locate a chapter of a relevant book or a journal article and read it using the SQ3R technique.

1. Survey – *leafing through the pages; noting the layout; looking at the headings and sub-headings used; reading the first and last sentences of main paragraphs; and examining any diagrams, familiarising yourself with the material.*

2. Question *yourself about the structure. What questions should you keep in mind while reading?*

3. Read *actively and quickly, looking to identify the main points.*

4. Recall *and write down the main points, together with any important facts and opinions. How would you reference a direct quotation from this text.*

5. Review, *repeat stages 1–3, amending your notes if necessary. Where in your assessments can you use this information?*

Summary

In this chapter you have learned about:

- researching using different media

- choosing and evaluating texts and other resources

- reading texts actively and critically

Theory focus

Books

Denby, N., Butroyd, R., Swift, H., Price, J. and Glazzard, J. (2008) *Master's level study in education: A guide to success for PGCE students*. Maidenhead: OUP.

Fleming, N. (2005), *Teaching and learning styles: VARK strategies*. Honolulu: Honolulu Community College.

Honey, P. and Mumford, A. (1992) *The manual of learning styles*, (3rd Edn.) Maidenhead: Peter Honey Associates.

Rowntree, D. (1998) *Learn how to study: A realistic approach*. London: Time Warner Books.

Williams, J. (2010) *Study Skills for PTLLS*, (1st Edn.) London: Learning Matters.

Websites

Alta Visa (search engine)	http://uk.altavista.com
Ask Jeeves (search engine)	http://uk.ask.com
BeCal (information gateway)	www.becal.net
BUBL Information Service (information gateway)	www.bubl.ac.uk
Citeulike (academic-focused online social bookmarking tool)	www.citeulike.org
Connotea (academic-focused online social bookmarking tool)	www.connotea.org
Delicious (online social bookmarking tool)	http://delicious.com
Diigo (online social bookmarking tool)	www.diigo.com
Eurydice at NFER	www.nfer.ac.uk/eurydice
Excellence Gateway (LSIS) (information gateway)	www.excellencegateway.org.uk
Google (search engine)	www.google.co.uk
Google e-bookstore	http://books.google.com/ebooks?uid=117522004192189783614&as_coll=1040
H20 Playlist (academic online social bookmarking tool)	http://h2obeta.law.harvard.edu
Hathi Trust	www.hathitrust.org/
IngentaConnect (online journal abstracts and articles)	www.ingentaconnect.com
Intute (information gateway)	www.intute.ac.uk
LibraryThing (books-focused online social bookmarking tool)	www.librarything.com
Online Computer Library Center (Dewey) (OCLC)	www.oclc.org/dewey/about/default.htm
Open Library	http://openlibrary.org/
Project Gutenberg	www.gutenberg.org/
Questia	www.questia.com
Wikipedia	www.wikipedia.org
Yahoo! (search engine)	http://uk.yahoo.com

CHAPTER 4
REFLECTIVE PRACTICE AND REFLECTIVE LEARNING JOURNAL WRITING

Introduction

In this chapter you will learn about:

- reflecting on learning
- the reflective cycle
- writing reflective learning journal entries

There are activities and examples to help you reflect on the above which will assist your understanding of how to reflect on your learning and write meaningful reflective learning journal entries.

Reflecting on learning

Reflection is a skill which will continue to support your teaching and learning over your lifetime. Reflective learning is a purposeful activity; that is you reflect with a purpose to learn and apply something new, not simply to recall past events. It is an active process of exploration, questioning and self-discovery that takes time and practice to perfect. It involves open-mindedness in thinking through issues, asking questions, finding information and considering new perspectives; combining the outcomes of these will help you understand what you know and how to use it to greater effect. It works best when you think about your actions and experiences both during and after an event, and then look back at the past with a view to the future. If you take this one step further to reflect on your reflections, you move beyond reflective practice into reflexive practice, where you consider how your own values, beliefs and attitudes affect your thoughts and actions, and, therefore, other people.

In the words of Gutek (1997: 1)

When the teacher begins to reflect on his or her role, that person is beginning to pass from preoccupation with the immediately practical to an examination of the theory that underlies and sustains practice … Theory without practice is insufficient, practice unguided by theory is aimless.

While working towards your PTLLS Award you might be asked to think about how you can put the theory you study into practice, and to record your thoughts in a reflective learning journal (RLJ). Even if it isn't a mandatory part of your PTLLS Award, you might find keeping an RLJ very worthwhile. As its name suggests, your RLJ should not be a straightforward description of events and feelings, but an opportunity to evidence both your reflective thinking processes and the outcomes in terms of enhanced learning and improved teaching. Your RLJ is personal to you, and will reflect your personality and learning experiences through a written collection of observations, thoughts and ideas put together, on a regular basis, throughout the programme. Your RLJ doesn't need to be written in formal academic style, although it is good practice, especially at level 4, to include some citations and quotations (see Chapter 5). Be prepared to experiment and have fun with your RLJ and include lots of different styles, and types of information. It is a chance to take risks and experiment with your writing. Engage with your RLJ and make sure it includes thoughts, ideas and reflections that you will want to revisit. If you enjoy drawing, why not depict some of your reflections in drawings and cartoons? You might want to write some of your reflections in poetry, or to cut out and paste in relevant newspaper cuttings, pictures, or other notes. You could even keep your RLJ electronically, scanning in documents and images and even sound files (your own or other podcasts and recordings) to make it more meaningful. (Do check with your assessor first that this will be acceptable – you might need to plan so that you can print out an electronic copy, and include transcripts of any audio files.)

It can be very useful to keep a *Bring Forward* box or a file that is complementary to your RLJ. This is simply a box or file with partitions sequenced by date, possibly in months, where you can put snippets of information to be revisited at a future date. These might range from reading material that you don't have time to study at the moment, to details of a course that you want to take up in the following academic year.

Example

When he was reflecting about the need to embed numeracy into vocational subjects for his PTLLS Award, Aleksandar realised that he would need to brush-up his own numeracy skills. Straightaway he researched suitable courses, but he knew he wasn't going to have time to take a numeracy course at the same time as his PTLLS Award. With the PTLLS Award due to finish in July, he found details of a numeracy course starting in September, and filed them in his Bring Forward box in the August slot. In this way he would be reminded just in time to complete the application process and book the dates out in his new academic diary.

Reflection is an important skill to develop, with many benefits.

Reflective students tend to:

- be motivated, knowing what they are trying to achieve and why
- use existing knowledge and experience more readily to help understand new concepts
- build current learning on a critical evaluation of previous experiences
- be self-directed and self-aware, identifying and addressing their own strengths and areas for development

Reflection can be applied to any aspect of your teaching and learning from how you react to different situations to skills that you need to develop, from critical (i.e. significant incidents) to educational policy, from teaching and learning methods to the purpose of education. Anything and everything can be subjected to a reflective/reflexive gaze. By actively reflecting you move into a continuous cycle of learning, reflecting, evaluating and revising before you are ready to begin again on the processes of re-learning, reflecting, and so on.

The reflective cycle

Although many models of reflective/reflexive practice exist, there is no standard process. What is important is that you engage in open-minded and constructive self-analysis. The *7D Reflective Cycle* (Williams, 2010) provides a helpful way to structure your reflective practice, and a focus for beginning your RLJ. Begin with *Describe* (see Figure 4.1), and work through the model sequentially. Once you have completed the 'decide' phase, you are ready to start the cycle afresh equipped with new insights.

Figure 4.1 7D Reflective Cycle (Williams, 2010)

This model should help you to set out your reflective thoughts in a logical sequence and to identify ways of developing or changing your practice. It works for day-to-day incidents as well as for what can be termed as critical incidents. Day-to-day incidents take place all the time, for example, a student who always seems to do the absolute bare minimum to scrape through with a pass, and never seems to engage fully with any teaching and learning activity. What transforms a day-to-day incident into a critical one, Tripp (1993) suggests, is our value judgment of its significance, whether at the time it occurs or later in retrospect. At the time it might be assumed that the student is simply lazy or balancing competing priorities by doing only what must be done. In retrospect, a more alarming reason for the apparent lack of application might be discovered, making this a critical incident.

1. **Describe** how and why you did what you did or what happened. This can be a critical incident that you feel might have been better handled, for example, a student using inappropriate language in class, or an

aspect of your practice such as your approach to a group task during your PTLLS taught session. Be careful to write down not only *what* happened, but who was involved, *when* and *where* the event took place. This additional information might be significant when you consider later how and why the event occurred.

2. **Distinguish** the most useful or significant learning point. This is the most valuable thing that you believe you learned from the event. It might be something not related to the subject you were studying at the time, for example, how different another student's values, beliefs and attitudes on the subject were from your own, and those of others in the room.

3. **Determine** your thoughts and feelings and those of others when the event occurred. Think about how you felt at the time you noticed this. What emotions did you experience? What thoughts went through your mind? What, if anything, did others say? What happened to the body language in the group?

4. **Discriminate** positive and negative elements from differing viewpoints. When you do this try to view the episode through different *lenses*. Brookfield (1995) talks of the need to be critical when reflecting, looking at things not only from your own perspective, but also from the viewpoints of others involved, together with relevant reading and research.

5. **Dissect** the event into key points that make sense of the situation. *How* and *why* did the situation arise? What were the catalysts? What caused it to develop as it did?

6. **Debate** how it might have been managed differently. Could it have been prevented? What were the positive aspects of the way in which it was handled this time? In what different ways could it have been managed? Which aspects might have worked better/worse? Why?

7. **Decide** if it happens again what to keep and what to change. Remember when you do this that it is equally important when reflecting to identify strengths and behaviours that you would want to repeat, as those that need to be revised.

At this point you are ready to begin the cycle again, equipped with your new insights to use when a similar event happens in the future.

Activity

Use this cycle, or a similar one you have located in a relevant textbook, to focus upon your personal responses, reactions and reflections to new ideas and concepts that you have met recently through one of the following:

- *a lecture, seminar or workshop that you attended or delivered*

- *research and reading*

- *a discussion with your peers*

- *a critical incident that you experienced or observed.*

Writing reflective learning journal entries

It is important that you make time for writing your RLJ. Try to regularly set aside some time for reflection, writing down your thoughts as soon as possible after each PTLLS teaching session you have attended. Try to use the RLJ to help you to:

- identify the main points you have learned from the session

- step back, exploring and analysing your own role, thoughts and feelings

- consider potentially different perspectives of others involved

- determine advantages and disadvantages, strengths and areas for development

- make connections, where appropriate, with educational theories and research that support your ideas

- consider potential wider implications, e.g. for your organisation, local communities, local and national government, even international developments

- show awareness of social and political influences

- identify anything you find puzzling, difficult or contradictory, and work out how you might go about understanding it better

- record any *light bulb* moments, where something that was puzzling you suddenly becomes clear

- identify points you need to explore further, and ways to organise this

- identify practical skills for development and potential opportunities

- evaluate resources that have been particularly useful and/or interesting, thinking how you might be able to adapt them for your own use

- recognise new knowledge, skills or understanding you have gained

Sometimes you will find it very easy to start writing, prompted by an incident that you want to explore further. At other times it will be more difficult. You might find it helps to decide on a focus in advance of the lesson.

Example

When he is getting ready for his PTLLS session later in the day, Thane remembers from the plenary last week that the session is going to focus on the principles of assessment. He is particularly interested to find out more about the process of peer assessment because in his own learning experiences both at school and at college he remembered it to be dismally counter-productive. Because of this he had always shunned it and deliberately never used it in his teaching. He decides to use the session as an opportunity to talk to other group members and his teacher about their views and experiences. After the session he will work through each of the seven stages of the 7D Reflective Cycle (Williams, 2010), describing what happened during the session, distinguishing the key learning points, determining his reactions to these, and reflecting from differing perspectives (including new research and reading) to discriminate some positive and negative elements of peer assessment. Having done this he can dissect his findings to identify what made his own experiences so negative, and debate how these might have been differently managed to achieve a positive outcome. He will then decide, based on this reflection, how best to introduce elements of peer assessment into his own practice, making a note of these so that he can implement them with his group. He makes a note to ask his teacher to recommend one or two books that he could read on the subject. Now Thane has a focus for his RLJ he feels much happier that he will be able to produce a meaningful entry for the session.

Sometimes it can be useful to adopt metaphors to help you define and explore your reflections. Originating from the Greek meaning to *transfer*, a metaphor is a figure of speech which transfers meaning from one word, image or idea to another by comparison with different and unrelated things that actually have a fundamental likeness. Transferring a situation in this way can enable you to see it removed from conventional constraints, making it possible to examine and interpret thoughts and events differently.

Genuinely reflective writing might involve disclosing anxieties, failures, and areas for development, as well as successes and strengths, so using metaphors can make the process seem less intrusive, although you do need to remember to consider the possible causes and ways to address these.

For example, you might want to focus on the learning environment as:

- a garden, where teachers grow and cultivate green shoots of knowledge they plant within their students

- a fuel station, where the teacher as petrol pump attendant fills the student cars with petrol or diesel

- a pond, where the teacher skims the student stones and the ripples of water created are the boundless effects of teaching, some of which the teacher never sees (Adapted from Claxton, 1999, and Cole, 2008)

Example

Andrew attends a PTLLS session in which the group is studying learning styles. He had not known of the existence of learning styles theories before this session. The entry in his RLJ looks like this:

'I thought about a garden today, where some plants like camellias and azaleas are lime haters and need an acid soil, and others such as daffodils prefer more alkaline conditions. In fact daffodils absolutely need a pH higher than 7 and simply won't grow in acidic soil. I wouldn't dream of expecting my camellias to grow and flourish in my daffodil beds!

Today I found out that we all have preferred ways of learning, and that these can all be very different. I learned a lot about my own personal learning styles which are predominantly visual (Fleming, 2005) and reflector (Honey and Mumford, 1992).

Thinking about this has helped me to realise why sometimes I can't 'flourish' when I don't have the right soil – for example the teacher using the whiteboard or PowerPoint to reinforce things like difficult spellings and new terminology. I also understand better why some people have a tendency to jump in and answer questions straightaway, while I often take much longer before I am prepared to say anything. Because of this I shall be more patient with others for seeming to take over, and with myself for not making my voice heard.

Continued

What struck me most, however, were the different ways that I can adapt my own soil, changing material that is given to me to make it easier to learn – by using spider diagrams and concept maps, for example.

To make my use of spider diagrams and concept maps more effective, I am going to look on the internet for some of the free software that our teacher talked about. I think I would really enjoy using something like that, and it would mean that I could have fun and be creative reviewing my notes.

I'm also going to go over my notes again, and carry out some more research to make sure I really understand the meanings of all the learning styles we covered so that I am confident when I introduce the learning styles questionnaires to my own students. I'm also going to make a note in my Bring Forward box to investigate more different learning styles when I have time – after I have finished the PTLLS Award!'

Writing an RLJ also gives you the opportunity to consider your long-term development. You could ask yourself the following questions.

- Have you changed your beliefs, values or opinions during the experience?

- How can you improve your learning, thinking and working in the future?

- Have you identified the next step(s) for your further development?

As well as the benefits derived from reflective practice itself, the very process of keeping an RLJ has its own advantages.

- It provides a record of your growing understanding of the teaching process, and developing thoughts and ideas. You can look back on your RLJ over time to see the distance you have travelled.

- Writing something down often helps to bring it to life and helps to clarify thoughts.

- Making associations and links between different aspects and subjects aids memory.

- An RLJ should help you to identify and build on your strengths and recognize areas for development, and also your preferred learning (and teaching) styles.

Benita, a new teacher, sums up her reasons for writing an RLJ: 'I write in a journal to get my thoughts out and to reflect on my classroom practice. I write in a journal because it allows me to go back in time and read what I have written to see if I have come up with new insights and answers to my questions. My journal is a place where I can see how I have grown professionally' (cited in Craig 1995:83).

Remember to complete your RLJ regularly as you work through your PTLLS Award. In this way it will act as a tool to help your learning and progression, both when you are writing it, and in the future. Although it can be difficult to find time to reflect on an incident soon after it has happened, giving way to the temptation to leave it to the end of your PTLLS Award programme to put together some hastily reconstructed notes to serve the purpose will not only be frustrating, but unrewarding. If you don't make a note of something shortly after it happens, you might forget a significant occurrence, or an automatic reaction that you experienced, finding yourself unable to work out later exactly what it was that seemed important at the time. It is, of course, only natural to view an event differently and more rationally with the benefit of hindsight, and this too might stifle your reflectivity because, as Gutek (1997: 1) suggests, *one's view of reality shapes one's beliefs about knowledge*. If you can't make notes straightaway, for example, because you are driving home from a taught session, you could mentally run through a few points. You could consider what you learned and how you could put theory into practice. Or you could use a digital voice recorder or mobile phone to record your initial thoughts. It might help, later, to discuss your thoughts and ideas with others, engaging with their different perspectives and ideas, to help you to write a truly reflective learning journal.

Remember to always treat reflection and reflective practice as important and integral parts of your PTLLS Award and as part of the wider the learning process. After all, as Socrates (469–399 BC) states in the writing of his own epitaph – 'the unexamined life is not worth living' (BBC, 2005).

Summary

In this chapter you have learned about:

- reflecting on learning
- the reflective cycle
- writing reflective learning journal entries

Theory focus

Books

Brookfield, S. D. (1995) *Becoming a critically reflective teacher*, San Francisco: Jossey-Bass.

Claxton, G. (1999) *Wise-up*, London: Bloomsbury.

Craig, C. (1995) 'Coming to know on the professional knowledge landscape: Benita's first year of teaching', in Clandinin, D. J. and Connelly, F. M. (Eds.) *Teachers' professional knowledge landscapes*, New York: Teachers' College Press, Chapter 7: 79–87.

Gravells, A. (2012a) *Preparing to Teach in the Lifelong Learning Sector*, (5th Edn.) London: Learning Matters.

Gravells, A. (2012b) *Passing PTLLS Assessments*, (2nd Edn.) London: Learning Matters.

Gutek, G. (1997) *Philosophical and ideological perspectives on education*, 2nd edn. Boston: Allyn and Bacon.

Roffey-Barentsen, J. and Malthouse, R. (2009) *Reflective practice in the lifelong learning sector*, (2nd Edn.) Exeter: Learning Matters.

Tripp, D. (1993) *Critical incidents in teaching: Developing professional judgement*. Abingdon: Routledge.

Websites

BBC Radio 4 (2005)) Philosophy resource [Online] Available at www.bbc.co.uk/radio4/history/inourtime/greatest_philosopher_socrates.shtml

Cole, B. (2008) Teachers and teaching metaphors [Online] Available at www.slideshare.net/bcole/teachers-and-teaching-metaphors-presentation

Free maths and English training www.move-on.org.uk

Free ICT training http://learn.go-on.co.uk/

The Sheffield College
Hillsborough LRC
Telephone: 0114 260 2254

Introduction

In this chapter you will learn about:

- avoiding plagiarism

- using and setting out quotations and citations in your text

- setting out references in your reference list and bibliography

There are activities and examples to help you reflect on the above, which will assist your understanding of how to reference your work for the PTLLS Award.

Avoiding plagiarism

There are many different definitions of plagiarism. Essentially, plagiarism is about presenting someone else's work and allowing others to believe it is your own. Pears and Shields (2010: 1) describe it as *a specific form of cheating … generally defined as presenting someone else's work or ideas as your own*, and as *taking and using another person's thoughts, writings or inventions as your own without acknowledging or citing the source of the ideas and expressions* (2010: 92). They go on to caution that where that material is copyrighted, *plagiarism is illegal* (Pears and Shields, 2010: 92). The Joint Council for Qualifications (JCQ), which consists of AQA, City & Guilds, CCEA, Edexcel, OCR, SQA and WJEC, the seven largest qualifications providers in the UK (JCQ, 2008), define it as the *failure to acknowledge sources properly and/or the submission of another person's work as if it were the candidate's own* (JCQ, 2008). Carroll (2002: 9) confirms that plagiarism can occur whether or not it was intended, and is something done *for your own benefit*, while Plagarism.org (2012) who describe themselves as *one of the internet's predominant anti-plagiarism resources for educators and students alike* state that *plagiarism is an act of fraud [which] involves both stealing someone else's work and lying about it afterward*. Northedge (2005: 280) points out that detected plagiarism can not only adversely affect your course result, but, perhaps more importantly *it is also cheating yourself of the opportunity to learn*.

As well as through more obvious causes, such as paying for an assignment and passing it off as your own, plagiarism can happen if you:

- copy just one particular word or phrase

- copy word-for-word

- leave out quotation marks from a direct quotation

- closely imitate a text you have read

- cut and paste text from the internet

- use data or data analysis prepared by someone else

- use others' pictures, charts or diagrams

- use your own notes taken from a text, lecture, or electronic media that contain direct quotations

It is therefore best to consider that if you submit an assessment that contains an exact copy, paraphrasing, or other reproduction of anyone else's work, including their spoken or written words, pictures, figures, graphs or ideas (whether: published or not; for gain or not; intentionally or not), without *acknowledging your sources*, you are guilty of plagiarism.

- A *source* is any person, organisation or medium that you use to obtain information for your coursework, including not only textbooks and journals but media including newspapers, magazines, e-books, television and radio broadcasts, DVDs, videos, podcasts, pictures, charts, even a conversation with another person. It does not matter whether the information is free or paid for, and it also includes anything you might find on the internet.

- *Acknowledging* means mentioning the source alongside the relevant material in the body of your assignment, and including full details at the end of your writing that can be used to trace the original.

If you work with others on tasks that you are supposed to carry out individually, although this is not strictly considered plagiarism, it is equally unacceptable academic dishonesty or malpractice, which is often referred to as collusion.

When you submit your PTLLS Award final portfolio for certification, it will include at least one statement, signed by you, to confirm that all the work you have submitted is your own. As a part of this, you will be confirming that any sources you refer to in your work have been acknowledged, that you have not committed plagiarism or collusion.

So widespread is the concern about plagiarism that some learning providers use special software packages to detect it. They may check submitted papers without bringing this to your notice, or you might be asked to submit your work electronically through a plagiarism checking system such as Turnitin. There are also programs for students to use to check their own work for accidental plagiarism. These include free sites such as Dustball, Plagiarism Checker, and others such as WriteCheck (associated with Turnitin) who charge a nominal fee for their services which are delivered through a secure website. Website addresses are included in the Theory Focus at the end of this chapter and again in Appendix 5.

Various styles of referencing are used in academic work, and these fall into two main types:

- Author-date referencing (including HRS [Harvard Referencing Style], APA [American Psychological Association] and MLA [Modern Language Association]). These require author name(s) and year of publication to be inserted in the body of the text at the place of a citation or quotation, and full details to be included at the end of the assignment in a Reference list.

- Numeric referencing (including MHRA [Modern Humanities Research Association], OSCOLA [Oxford Standard for Citation of Legal Authorities] and Vancouver), which identifies each quotation or citation by a superscript number in the body of the text and includes full details in footnotes and bibliographies.

The Harvard style of referencing is the style that is generally used in the natural and social sciences, including education, and it is the style that is recommended for the PTLLS Award. According to Chernil (1988), the Harvard referencing style can be traced back to zoologist Edward Laurens Mark (1847–1946), Hersey professor of anatomy and director of Harvard's zoological laboratory until his retirement in 1921. On page 194 of a paper about the common garden slug, written by Mark and published in 1881, appears a parenthetic author-date citation, the first known evidence of the style (Chernil, 1988).

Advantages of the Harvard referencing style for the reader are that it is quick and easy when reading the text to see at a glance when particular arguments were made and by whom. Arguably it is also easier to read as the information is available in the flow of the the text in standard sized print, rather than outside the scope of the text and in a smaller font which often happens with the footnotes and endnotes of a numeric system. A primary disadvantage is that the insertion of this additional information in the body of the text can easily upset the flow of the writing.

If you are completing your PTLLS Award at level 3, it is good practice to include a bibliography at the end of your work – a list of all the books you have read that have informed your ideas about the subject, but that you have not directly mentioned. For details of how to do this, move on to the section later in this chapter headed: *Setting out references in your reference list and bibliography.*

If you are aiming to achieve your PTLLS Award at level 4, you will need to research and read various publications including books, journals, and electronic sources such as material from the internet, e-books, podcasts and CD-ROMs. You will then need to refer to these sources by directly quoting or paraphrasing (where you put the information into your own words) to provide evidence for any statements you make.

It is crucial that, when you do this, you pay careful attention to accurate referencing so that you can:

- show, in a standard system, sources of information and other people's ideas you have used

- acknowledge the work of the original authors

- find the sources again for your own future reference, and help others to find them

- ensure that you do not commit plagiarism

There are two steps to acknowledgement using Harvard referencing:

- Firstly, within your writing, you need to insert the author and the date of publication, together with the page number if you use a direct quotation.

- Secondly, at the end of your piece of writing, you need to include full details of all your information sources in a Reference list. (Examples of how to do this are included later in this chapter, under the heading: *Setting out references in your reference list and bibliography.*)

Using and setting out quotations and citations in your text

You should use references in the body of your text to support and confirm your statements, showing that the information you are giving has a background and credibility.

Example

Tasha is completing an assignment about ground rules. She wants to argue that it is important to involve learners in the setting of these, and that doing so pays dividends in group behaviour. She therefore looks for a phrase or sentence in a textbook to support this argument, and then writes as follows:

This enables your students to recognise what is and what is not acceptable, giving them "a sense of ownership and responsibility ... and encourages aspects such as listening, compromise and respect for others" (Gravells, 2012: 93).'

Sometimes, as in Tasha's example, you might wish to leave out part of a quotation (be careful, if you do, not to change the meaning). In such a case you can use an ellipsis, three evenly spaced dots with a space either side, as Tasha has done, to show where words have been left out.

Occasionally you will want to use a direct quotation that includes an error, misspelling or other anomaly. Because you are quoting, you need to be faithful to the original text, but you might want to draw your reader's attention to the fact that this was in the original text. To do this, you insert [sic] immediately after quoted word. From the Latin meaning 'so, thus' it is used to show that the word appeared this way in the original. In the example from the Excellence Gateway that follows, the writer's own words are faithfully reproduced, possibly to show some of the difficulties that can occur with dyslexia: 'It has helped me realise that I have dyslexia and that I can get help with my readying [sic] and spelling which I have difficulty with at college' (Excellence Gateway, 2009).

You can also introduce your own words into a quotation for clarification by including them in square brackets, and emphasise words by putting them into italics.

Example

Harry wants to use part of a quotation from Gravells (2012a) to evidence his writing about supporting learners with specific issues, needs and concerns. The sentence that he would like to use doesn't stand alone as it includes a pronoun (their) that isn't linked to a subject in the same sentence. To make this work, he inserts the phrase the students' *in square brackets after the pronoun to clarify the meaning:*

'In such a case Gravells (2012a: 51) recommends asking "if there is anything you could do to help to make their [the students'] experience a more positive one."'

If you are using a quotation that is already showing emphasis by use of italics, underlining, or emboldening of text, it is a good idea to make this clear by including the words *emphasis in the original* immediately afterwards.

Example

In a short article she is writing to go with her presentation, Ananaya includes the following:

Baron-Cohen (2004: 53) asserts that while men often use language to demonstrate knowledge, skill and status, women are more concerned with making others feel listened to. They will often compliment each other very soon after meeting: 'Oh, I love *your dress. You* must *tell me where you got it. You look* so *pretty in it.' (emphasis shown by underlining).*

Paraphrasing

When you paraphrase, you put someone else's text into your own words. This serves several purposes when you working towards your PTLLS Award.

- Accurate paraphrasing demonstrates your understanding of the material.

- Paraphrasing helps your writing to flow seamlessly from paragraph to paragraph.

- Writing in your own words helps you to start to develop your own writing 'voice' – your own distinctive writing style – which will become increasingly important if you decide to progress from PTLLS to CTLLS or DTLLS or other qualifications involving academic writing.

- Because you are engaging more actively with the text, you are far more likely to remember what you have written. (See also Chapter 3 for information on reading and remembering.)

When you paraphrase, you must be very careful not to change the author's meaning, and you must cite (include details of) your source in Harvard format both in your text and in your Reference list at the end of your writing. Paraphrasing involves far more than just changing one or two words in a sentence with the help of the computer thesaurus, which would leave you open to accusations of plagiarism.

Example

Becky wants to work out exactly what differentiation in teaching is about, so that she can use differentiation effectively herself, and so that she can answer an assessment question. She has been reading **Preparing to teach in the lifelong learning** *sector by Ann Gravells, where she finds a useful ten-line paragraph on page 73. It is late and she is exhausted, so it's very tempting to just copy the first four lines, putting them in quotation marks and acknowledging them with the author's surname, date and page number to avoid plagiarism. However, because she wants to make sure that it is clear from her writing that she understands this topic, and because she wants to be able to use differentiation effectively with her own students, she takes some time to read over the paragraph carefully several times, deciding on the key points and working out exactly what the text means. (SQ3R mentioned in Chapter 3 would help with this.) Finally, she turns the book face down and writes her own interpretation. When she has done this she compares her own version with the book to make sure the meaning is the same. When she is satisfied she enters her final version into her assignment, attributing the source to the book she has read:*

'Because every student in a class is likely to be at a different ability level, with different backgrounds, learning and needs, a successful teacher will use a range of approaches, methods and resources in an attempt to make learning accessible to everyone (Gravells, 2012a).'

(Becky has included the letter a after the date in her reference to Gravells's work because she has also referred to another book by Gravells also published in 2012, Passing PTLLS assignments, which she has labelled b in her text and her reference list so as to clearly distinguish between the two.)

Becky will go back to her writing in a couple of days' time, to see whether she can improve the way it reads, without changing its meaning.

When you paraphrase or summarise someone else's work, you should always include the author's name and date in the main body of your text.

- *One author*: include the surname and the date. For example, where the author's name is used in the structure of the sentence: *Williams (2012) points out the crucial nature of accurate referencing,* or, where the author's name is not used in the sentence: *Accurate referencing is crucial* (Williams, 2012).

- *Up to three authors*: include all surnames, and the date – for example, *(Gravells and Simpson, 2009).*

- *Four or more authors*: use the surname of the first author, followed by *et al.* – for example, *(Coffield et al., 2004).* The term *et al.* is Latin, meaning 'and others'. (All authors must be acknowledged in your Reference list.)

Where you use a direct quotation, you must also include the page number, and, if there are up to two or three lines, place speech marks around the words that you are quoting: 'You need to remain in control, be fair and ethical with all your students and not demonstrate any favouritism' (Gravells, 2012: 16). Longer quotations should be introduced by a colon and indented into the text, in single-line spacing, without quotation marks:

A scheme of work (sometimes referred to as a learning programme) is a document used to structure the teaching of your subject in a progressive way. It can be for a whole programme or just a unit of a qualification and can be amended at any time if necessary (Gravells, 2012: 62).

Use long quotations sparingly, and only to support your statements. Some assessors might consider a student who uses long quotations to be lazy; simply not making the effort to understand and re-word the text themselves. You may also have a word limit when responding to questions. Equally importantly, putting the material into your own words helps you to remember it better and to fashion your own writing style.

Sometimes, you will use a quotation where the author of a book or other publication quotes someone else. This is known as a secondary citation. For example, Gravells and Simpson use this quotation from the Tomlinson Report (1996): '*By inclusive learning we mean the greatest degree of match or fit between how learners learn best, what they need and want to learn ...*'

● *Secondary citation*: use the surname(s) of the original author and date *cited in* the name of the current author(s), date and page number. For example, (Tomlinson, 1996, cited in Gravells and Simpson, 2009: 34).

The details of Gravells' and Simpson's book appear in the Reference list at the end of the writing, but without mention of Tomlinson. Wherever possible, however, rather than using a secondary citation, you should try to find and refer to the original work.

Where an item has no author, you should include the title, instead of the author's name, and where there is no date available, enter (*date unknown*). In such a case, however, it is worth thinking very carefully about the value of such a source as evidence to support your writing.

Sometimes, an author has two or more publications in the same year. These should be differentiated by including a sequential lowercase letter after the date of each in the body of the text, and again in the Reference list at the end. An example of this can be seen with Gravells' two books published in 2012 and referred to in this book: *Preparing to teach in the lifelong sector* (Gravells, 2012a) and *Passing PTLLS Assessments* (Gravells, 2012b).

Setting out references in your reference list and bibliography

A Reference list contains details of all the information sources mentioned in your writing. A Bibliography details the sources you have accessed during the study process, but have not referred to in your writing. Usually only one or the other is needed but, if you do include both, sources mentioned in the Reference list should *not* appear again in the Bibliography. Both are arranged alphabetically by author's surname and comprise separate pages at the end of your writing. Publication titles should be in italics, or underlined if you are handwriting, and either be in title case – where the first word and every other significant word are capitalised – or with only the first word of the title capitalised (see examples that follow):

Title case	*A Handbook for Deterring Plagiarism in Higher Education*
First word capitalised	*A handbook for deterring plagiarism in higher education*

Where you refer to a book, if it is a second or later edition, you also need to include the edition number after the title. Always be consistent with your layout and punctuation throughout.

Sometimes you will want to reference work from journals or other periodicals. Journals are made up of issues, usually produced at regular intervals; for example, monthly, quarterly, or annually, which are combined into volumes for a given period; for example, a calendar or academic year. The sequence for volume, issue and pages can be remembered as VIP.

When referencing a website, the author's name and date should be given, together with a title if possible and the full internet address of the page you visited, not the home page. The date you accessed the site should also be included. It is not generally necessary to separate websites from other media; they should be included in alphabetical order by author surname or, if no name is available, by title.

Some learning providers have their own *house style* that they prefer their students to use, which might differ slightly from the guidelines in this book. For example, the house style used in this series of books is to italicise all quotations and omit quotation marks regardless of their length. It is always a good idea, for this reason, to check with your assessor before you start writing to see if there are any set differences that you need to observe. However, they will probably be much more focused on seeing that your presentation is consistent throughout a piece of work, than on checking that you have followed minute detail.

Example

Books

Books with one author

Surname, Initials. (Year) *Book title in italics*, Place (city or town) of publication: Name of Publisher.

Williams, J. (2012) *Study Skills for PTLLS*, (2nd Edn.) London: Learning Matters.

Books with two or more authors

Surname, Initials., Surname, Initials. and Surname, Initials. (Year) *Book title in italics*, Place (city or town) of publication: Name of Publisher.

Vella, J., Berardinelli, P. and Burrow, J. (1998) *How do they know they know: evaluating adult learning*, San Francisco: Jossey-Bass Publishers.

Edited books

Surname, Initials. (ed) (Year) *Book title in italics*, Place (city or town) of publication: Name of Publisher.

Desforges, C. (ed) (1995) *An introduction to teaching*, Oxford: Blackwell Publishers.

Chapters in edited books

Surname of chapter author, Initials. (Year) 'Chapter title' in Initials and Surname of Editor of Book (ed) *Book Title in italics*, (Chapter number and page range), Place (city or town) of publication: Name of Publisher.

Kirkup, G. and Jones, A. (1996) 'New technologies for open learning: the superhighway to the learning society?' in P. Raggatt, R. Edwards and N. Small (eds) *The learning society: challenges and trends*, Chapter 17, 272–291, London: Routledge.

Electronic books (e-books)

Surname, Initials. (Year) *Book title in italics*, *Name of e-book collection in italics*, [Online] Available at path address (date accessed).

Dawson, C. (2006) Returning to learning. *How to Books*, [Online] Available at **www.howto.co.uk/learning/adult-learning/** (Accessed 10/02/2012)

Publication dates may vary between printed books and their e-versions. Always use the date of the e-version you are using.

Continued

Government publications

Command Papers including Green and White Papers

Great Britain. Name of committee or Royal Commission (Year) *Title in italics*. **Place (city or town) of Publication: Name of Publisher (Paper number).**

Great Britain. House of Commons Education and Skills Committee (2003) *Every Child Matters*. London: The Stationery Office (CM5860).

Departmental Publications

Country. Department (Year) *Report title in italics*, **(Chairman:), Place (city or town) of publication: Name of Publisher. (Series in brackets – if applicable).**

Great Britain. DfEE (1999) *Improving literacy and numeracy: A fresh start: The report of the working group* (Chairman: Sir Claus Moser), London: DfEE Publications.

Journal articles

Journal articles

Surname, Initials of author/editor/journalist. (Year) 'Article Title', *Journal title in italics* [capitalise the first letter of each word except for linking words such as and, of, the, for], **Volume in italics (Issue number): Page range.**

Scheurich, J. J. (1994) 'Policy archaeology; a new policy studies methodology', *Journal of Education Policy*, 9 (4): 297–316.

Journal articles online

Surname, Initials of author/editor/journalist. (Year) 'Article Title', *Journal title in italics* [*capitalise the first letter of each word except for linking words such as and, of, the, for*], **Volume (Issue number): Page range Name of collection [Online] Available at path address (date accessed).**

Reis, S. M., McCoach, D. B., Little, C. A., Muller, L. M. and Kaniskan, R. B. (2011) 'The effects of differentiated instruction and enrichment pedagogy on reading achievement in five elementary schools', *American Educational Research Journal*, 48 (2): 462–501 Sage Journals [Online] Available at **http://aer.sagepub.com/content/48/2/462.abstract** (Accessed 10/02/2012).

Newspaper articles

Surname, Initials of author/editor/journalist. (Year) 'Article Title', *Journal title in italics* [*capitalise the first letter of each word except for linking words such as and, of, the, for*], **(Edition if required), Day, Month, Page.**

Whitehouse, R. (2012) 'School funding to drop by 20%', *Cornish Guardian* (North Cornwall), 8th February, p.15.

As above, you will need to include the region (edition) if you are referring to a regional, rather than national, newspaper.

Continued

Podcasts

Surname, Initials of author/presenter. (Year) 'Podcast title', *Title of internet site in italics* [Podcast] Day/Month of posted message, Available at path address (date accessed).

Abrams, F. (2011) 'Unsure about Sure Start', *BBC Radio 4 Analysis* [Podcast] 17th July, Available at **www.bbc.co.uk/programmes/b012fc5q** (Accessed 10/02/2012).

Although podcasts are frequently downloaded to an MP3 player or iPod (data storage that allows audio files to be reduced to about 10 per cent of their normal size without significant loss of quality, and listened to on the move), you should always make a note of (and acknowledge) the original source.

Printed learning materials

You should avoid direct reference to printed learning materials given to you during taught sessions, unless they have been issued in place of a textbook. Printed learning materials should be used as a guide to further independent reading.

Video or film on video cassette, DVD/Blu-ray

***Title of film in italics* (Year) Directed by Director [Video cassette] or [DVD] or [Blu-ray] Place of distribution: distribution company.**

What's eating Gilbert Grape (1993) Directed by Lasse Hallstrom [DVD] LA, California: Paramount Pictures.

Video or film on YouTube

Name of author/presenter. (Year) *Title of film in italics*, Available at path address (date accessed).

Shokthx (2010) *How to update or install Adobe Flash – Windows 7*, Available at **http://youtu.be/qL2mmSSfKks** (Accessed 10/02/2012).

Websites

Surname, Initials. (Year) *Article title in italics* [Online] (updated) Available at path address (date accessed).

Department for Education (2012) *Major overhaul to reform family justice system* [Online] (updated 06/02/2012) Available at **www.education.gov.uk/inthenews/ inthenews/a00203059/major-overhaul-to-reform-family-justice-system** (Accessed 10/02/2012).

In this last example, the author is an organisation: Department for Education (DfE). This website clearly shows the last date it was updated, and so this is included in the reference. If it had not been available, this part of the reference would have been left out.

Finding the date that a website was created or last updated can be difficult. These dates are sometimes displayed at the top of or at the foot of the web page. If not, there are a couple of other options that you can try.

1. With some browsers, if you right-click anywhere in blank space on a web page you get a menu that includes an item called *Page Info* or *View Page Info*. Figure 5.1 shows this in the Firefox browser. When you click on this, you get another tab (Figure 5.2) giving the required information.

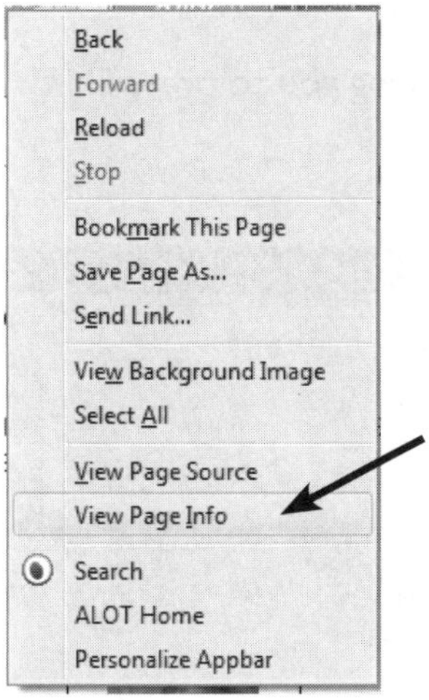

Figure 5.1 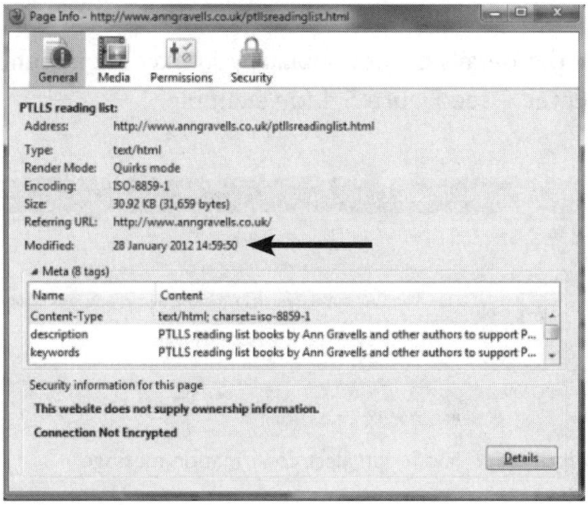   **Figure 5.2**

2. If this doesn't happen, clear the content from your browser window. (A browser is software used to navigate the internet such as Google Chrome, Firefox, Microsoft Internet Explorer, Opera and Safari, and the window is where the URL or web address appears.) This method will not work at the moment with Google Chrome as it strips out Javascript automatically, but it is working for Internet Explorer, Opera and Safari. Once you have deleted the web address, paste the following code into the space: *javascript:alert(document.lastModified)*, being careful not to leave any spaces on either side of this code – then press return. A box should appear – see Figure 5.3 for an example using a Safari browser. Note the use of the American date format: mm/dd/year. Unfortunately, cutting and pasting doesn't always work and you sometimes need to type the address into the window to get a result.

Figure 5.3 Web page last updated

If the details do not appear, you may get a menu asking you to press Shift + Enter – see Figure 5.4 for example.

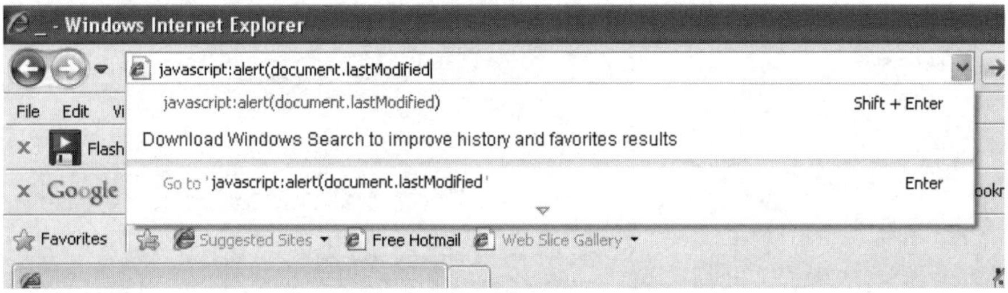

Figure 5.4 JavaScript: alert confirmation message

When you press Shift + Enter, a message should pop up (see Figure 5.3) showing you the date and time when the page was last updated.

For this to work, JavaScript must be enabled for your browser. JavaScript is a programming language designed to add interactivity and extra functionality to web pages. It is an open language that anyone can use without the need for a licence and it works in all major web browsers. The JavaScript code will then work for all web pages providing static content – where pages accessed by different users at different times are always the same. It will not work with dynamic web pages – which continually update information as pages are displayed. In the latter case, it will display the current date and time.

Missing information

- Where an item has no author, it is ordered in the reference list by the first significant word of the title, and the title is included instead of the author name, in the body of the text.

- Where an item has no date, in the brackets you should write (*date unknown*).

However, before using a source which has no obvious author or is undated, you do need to think carefully about its value in your work. (For further information on evaluating resources, see Chapter 3.)

Further reading

If you have read other sources, but not paraphrased or quoted them directly in the text, this *wider reading* can be included in a separate list, set out in exactly the same format, headed *Bibliography* or *Further Reading*.

In a book, the publishing information that you need can usually be found on the back of the title page. In journals, it is usually on the inside page. For websites, you need to ensure that you use the Uniform Resource Locator (URL) or address for the *page* that you consult, not the website's *Home* page. (For further information about website addresses, see Chapter 3.)

It will save you a great deal of time and work if you collect the full information needed for referencing at the time that you access or first read the publication, rather than try to track it down later. To help you with this, when you are researching for your assessment, keep the following summary at hand. It will remind you of what's needed for the most commonly used sources to make sure you collect all the information you need for your in-text citations and your Reference list.

You might find it useful to keep all your references information in a table in Microsoft Word at the end of your assessment, or in a separate document specifically set up for that purpose.

Reference details check list

Note:
Q signifies this information is needed for direct quotations

	Author(s)	Editor(s)	Year	Article title	Publication title	Edition	Town or City	Publisher	Issue information	Page numbers	Web address	Date last accessed
Book	✓		✓		✓	✓	✓	✓		✓ Q		
Edited book		✓	✓		✓	✓	✓	✓		✓ Q		
Chapter from an edited book	✓	✓	✓	✓	✓	✓	✓	✓		✓		
E-book	✓		✓		✓	✓		✓		✓ Q	✓	✓
Journal article	✓		✓	✓	✓				✓	✓ Q		
Electronic Journal article	✓		✓	✓	✓				✓	✓	✓	✓
Newspaper article	✓		✓	✓	✓				✓	✓		
Film or Video on YouTube	✓		✓		✓						✓	✓
Website	✓		✓		✓						✓	✓

Example

Ethan has decided to keep his reference list for his PTLLS Award work in four separate Word documents, one for each unit. He creates the first document: My_PTLLS_References_RRR, and inserts a table with nine columns, making sure that he keeps author names in a dedicated column, surname first, so that later he can sort them automatically into alphabetical order.

Author(s)	Year	Publication title	Edition	Town or City	Publisher	Article title, issue information, page numbers	Web address	Date accessed
Gravells, A.	2012	Preparing to teach in the lifelong learning sector	5th	London:	Learning Matters			
Gravells, A.	2012	Passing PTLLS Assessments	2nd	London:	Learning Matters			
Williams, J.	2012	Study skills for PTLLS	2nd	London:	Learning Matters			

This can then be automatically sorted into alphabetical order, saving you time and effort. If you prefer to handwrite your notes, you could enter your references by author surname or first significant word of the title in a feint ruled A-Z notebook, or in a binder with A-Z dividers. Whichever format you choose to use, keeping a log of useful sources is a good practice to develop from the beginning of your PTLLS Award programme.

If you are planning to achieve PTLLS at level 4, and intending to move on quite quickly to CTLLS or DTLLS, you might want to think about using software such as Zotero, a free Firefox extension or EndNote Web, a free web-based service, which helps you collect, manage and cite your research sources. With EndNote Web you can:

- collect and store reference information quickly and easily from online data

- access your references from anywhere (subject to internet access)

- share references with other EndNote Web users to simplify collaboration

- easily transfer references to or from EndNote Web on your desktop

- use 'Cite While You Write' in Microsoft Word to automatically insert and format references

A range of commercial programs is also available, including other EndNote products which have even greater functionality.

Activity

Try out your referencing skills

Question 1. This is the reference for Gravells' book in John's bibliography. Tick or cross the correct number for each part of this reference in the table below.

Extract from John's assessment

Gravells (2012: 33) states that "it is always useful to get your students to carry out a learning styles test".

Gravells, A. (2012) Preparing to teach in the lifelong learning sector (5th edn) London: Learning Matters

	1	2	3	4	5	6
Surname of the writer of the book	☐	☐	☐	☐	☐	☐
Publisher's name	☐	☐	☐	☐	☐	☐
Name of the book	☐	☐	☐	☐	☐	☐
Place of publication	☐	☐	☐	☐	☐	☐
Year of publication	☐	☐	☐	☐	☐	☐
The writer's initial(s)	☐	☐	☐	☐	☐	☐

Continued

Question 2. Emma has used the internet to research her assessment. Tick or cross the correct number for each part of the reference in the table below.

Petty, G. (2004) Active learning [Online] Available at www.geoffpetty.com/ activelearning.html (Accessed 2 February 2012)

	1	2	3	4	5	6
Year of publication on the internet	☐	☐	☐	☐	☐	☐
Author's initials	☐	☐	☐	☐	☐	☐
Website address (URL)	☐	☐	☐	☐	☐	☐
Surname of author	☐	☐	☐	☐	☐	☐
Name of the article	☐	☐	☐	☐	☐	☐
Date that Emma accessed the internet site	☐	☐	☐	☐	☐	☐

Question 3. What does (ed) mean in this entry in Hasina's References section?

Desforges, C. (ed) (1995) **An introduction to teaching,** *Oxford: Blackwell Publishers*

Edition .... ☐

Education .... ☐

Editor .... ☐

Question 4. What does (edn) mean in this entry of Ilona's References section?

Gravells, A. (2012) **Preparing to teach in the lifelong learning sector** *(5th edn), London: Learning Matters*

Edition .... ☐

Education ...... ☐

Editor .... ☐

Continued

Question 5. What is the difference between a References section and a Bibliography?

References include only those books, journals, articles, etc., that you have used for quotations and citations .... ☐

References will be shorter than a Bibliography .... ☐

Bibliography includes everything you have read and looked at for the assessment, even if you have not used it for quotations and citations .... ☐

A Bibliography will be a longer list than a Reference list .... ☐

Question 6. A direct quotation of two lines or fewer is encased in double quotation marks and remains within the body of the text. How should a direct quotation that is longer than two lines be presented?

In exactly the same format as a shorter one .... ☐

Inset into the text, single-line spaced, without any quotation marks, but preceded by a colon .... ☐

Inset into the text, in the same line spacing as the rest of the text, without quotation marks .... ☐

Encased in double quotation marks, inset into the text, in single line spacing .... ☐

Now look at Appendix 2 for the correct answers.

Summary

In this chapter you have learned about:

- avoiding plagiarism

- using and setting out quotations and citations in your text

- setting out references in your reference list and bibliography

Theory focus

Books

Baron-Cohen, S. (2004) *The essential difference*, London: Penguin Books.

Carroll, J. (2002) *A handbook for deterring plagiarism in higher education*, Oxford: Oxford Brookes University.

Chernil, E. (1988) 'The "Harvard system": A mystery dispelled', *British Medical Journal*. October 22,1062–1063 [Online] available at www.ncbi.nlm.nih.gov/pmc/articles/PMC1834803/pdf/bmj00308-0078.pdf

Coffield, F., Moseley, D., Hall, E. and Ecclestone, K. (2004) *Learning styles and pedagogy in post-16 learning: A systematic and critical review* [Online] Available at https://crm.lsnlearning.org.uk/user/order.aspx?code=041543 (Accessed 28/01/2012)

Dawson, C. (2006) Returning to learning. *How to Books*. [Online] Available at www.howto.co.uk/learning/adult-learning/ (Accessed 10/02/2012)

Desforges, C. (ed) (1995) *An introduction to teaching*, Oxford: Blackwell Publishers.

DfEE, (1999) *Improving literacy and numeracy: A fresh start: The report of the working group* (Chairman: Sir Claus Moser), London: DfEE Publications.

Gravells, A. (2012a) *Preparing to Teach in the Lifelong Learning Sector*, (5th Edn.) London: Learning Matters.

Gravells, A. (2012b) *Passing PTLLS Assessments*, (2nd Edn.) London: Learning Matters.

Gravells, A. and Simpson, S. (2012) *Equality and Diversity in the Lifelong Learning Sector*, (2nd Edn.) London: Learning Matters.

Kirkup, G. and Jones, A. (1996) 'New technologies for open learning: the superhighway to the learning society?' in P. Raggatt, R. Edwards and N. Small (eds) *The learning society: challenges and trends*, Chapter 17, 272–291. London: Routledge.

Northedge, A. (2005) *The good study guide*, (2nd Edn.) Milton Keynes: The Open University.

Pears, R. and Shields, G. (2010) *Cite them right: The essential referencing guide*, Basingstoke: Palgrave Macmillan.

Scheurich, J. J. (1994) 'Policy archaeology; a new policy studies methodology', *Journal Of Education Policy*, 9 (4): 297–316.

Vella, J., Berardinelli, P. and Burrow, J. (1998) *How do they know they know*, San Francisco: Jossey-Bass Publishers.

Williams, J. (2012) *Study Skills for PTLLS*, (2nd Edn.) London: Learning Matters.

Websites

Abrams, F. (2011) 'Unsure about Sure Start', *Analysis* [Podcast] 17th July, Available at www.bbc.co.uk/programmes/b012fc5q (Accessed 10/02/2012).

AQA [Online] Available at www.aqa.org.uk

CCEA [Online] Available at www.rewardinglearning.org.uk

City & Guilds [Online] Available at www.cityandguilds.com

Department for Education (2012) *Major overhaul to reform family justice system* [Online] (updated 06/02/2012) Available at www.education.gov.uk/inthenews/inthenews/a00203059/major-overhaul-to-reform-family-justice-system (Accessed 10/02/2012)

Dustball Plagiarism Checker [Online] Available at www.dustball.com/cs/plagiarism.checker/

Edexcel [Online] Available at www.edexcel.com

EndNote Web [Online] Available at www.endnote.com

Excellence Gateway (2009) *Dyslexic learners* [Online] Available at www.excellencegateway.org.uk/page.aspx?o=BSFAdyslexia

JCQ (2008) *Plagiarism in examinations* [Online] Available at www.jcq.org.uk/attachments/published/672/Plagiarism%20in%20Examinations%20FINAL.pdf

OCR [Online] Available at www.ocr.org.uk

Petty, G. (2004) *Active learning* [Online] Available at www.geoffpetty.com/activelearning.html

Plagiarism.org [Online] Available at www.plagiarism.org/plag_article_what_is_plagiarism.html

Plagiarism Checker [Online] Available at www.plagiarismchecker.com/

Shokthx (2010) *How to update or install Adobe Flash – Windows 7*, Available at http://youtu.be/qL2mmSSfKks (Accessed 10/02/2012).

SQA [Online] Available at www.sqa.org.uk

Turnitin *Originality Check and Grade Mark* [Online] Available at www.turnitin.com

WJEC [Online] Available at www.wjec.co.uk

WriteCheck (2012) *Improve your writing, avoid accidental plagiarism* [Online] Available at https://www.writecheck.com/static/home.html (note that the s in the http part of the address indicates a secure site).

Zotero (2012) Zotero [Online] Available at www.zotero.org

Introduction

In this chapter you will learn about:

- Presenting your work in writing

  - deciding on a structure

  - getting your ideas onto paper

  - using pictures, charts, etc., to support your writing

  - formal writing

- Presenting your work in practice

  - preparing for your micro-teach

  - effective presentations

  - information communication technology

There are activities and examples to help you reflect on the above which will assist your understanding of how to present your work in writing and in practice.

Presenting your work in writing

Deciding on a structure

Before you start writing any text for formal assessment, you should produce a general outline and plan a timeline for completion. You should be given a deadline for submission; try to be ahead of this so that you are not rushing your work. You will need to read the question carefully, two or three times, to establish:

- the submission date

- if there is a word count, and if not, roughly how many words will be needed to meet the criteria

- exactly what the question requires; for example, a reflective account with examples from your own practice, a hypothetical case study or a written response to a question

- the mode of final presentation; for example, academic writing, a summary or a table

- whether you will need to include pictures and/or charts

- whether you must word-process your work

- the meaning of the question – a range of different verbs is used in the assessment questions, each requiring a specific approach; for example, *describe* or *analyse*

Activity

How many of these words can you find in the word search, which includes some of the verbs commonly used in assessment questions? As you find each word, think about its meaning, and the type of information you might be required to include in your response.

(The answers to the word search are in Appendix 3.)

```
i t r n e d n r c x y x y t a e s
p i r d s t e o o i f f e c r e i
l a e n i u a l l u i y l l e e t
i n l i i s m t i t t y e i v y i
a s i a e a c m s v n l n m i e t
a s i e v a l u a t e n i f e d r
n e s c t a j p s r d r m n w i n
r a e e i e n a x s i e a a e e i
e r n x s e r a a e l s x p a a c
i e n p e t m p l i l e e r m i n
i m t l n y u i r y u n l c r o t
e c r o t m s e d e s c r i b e c
n l c r i t i q u e t e l p m o c
c x o e c u d o r p r n y i e y r
e s y l a n a y l l a c i t i r c
t e s e r u c e t v t e i c r e e
w i t i d t r c r s e e t i a t t
```

analyse	compare	complete	contrast
critically analyse	critique	define	deliver
describe	discuss	evaluate	examine
explain	explore	identity	illustrate
interpret	justify	list	outline
produce	review	state	summarise

(puzzle created using www.armoredpenguin.com)

Hopefully you are now familiar with the assessment terminology, and have given some thought to the type of information you might need to include to address the assessment questions.

Example

Jenny has to write a short account with the title 'Justify the approaches to learning and teaching you took in your micro-teach'. She describes what she did, giving logical reasons to support these decisions. Because she is aiming to achieve at level 4, she includes citations and quotations in her writing.

My lesson was on a practical skill; making a leather mobile phone pouch. Following Petty (2009) I incorporated different learning activities to make my teaching varied and interesting to learners with different learning styles. I used a didactic style to share the aim and objectives with my learners so that they knew what they were aiming for and could take some personal responsibility. I then moved onto demonstration with voiceover. This meant I could both explain and demonstrate the process, hence appealing to visual and auditory learners. Finally, I facilitated a 'hands on' activity where each learner made their own pouch. Not only did this appeal to kinaesthetic learners, but according to a study carried out in the mid-1960s and attributed to the National Training Laboratories in Maine, learners can retain 90 per cent of their learning by immediate use of learning. I also encouraged them to help each other during this part of the activity as a means for them to 'understand the method' (Petty, 2009: 253).

Table 6.1 overleaf gives a summary of other verbs you are likely to come across in assessment questions, together with their meanings.

Verb	Action required
Analyse	Separate (a topic) into its main parts or important features, including their relationship to each other, and present these clearly in your own words.
Clarify	Make simple and clear.
Comment on	Give your opioion or point of view.
Compare	Examine and emphasise similarities (between two or more topics), showing that you are aware of minor points of difference within areas of general similarity.
Complete	Bring (a topic) to a full conclusion, closing any gaps.
Consider	State your own thoughts.
Contrast	Examine and emphasise the differences (between two or more topics).
Critically analyse or critique	Analyse the different aspects (of a topic), giving your opinion about merits and shortcomings. You should support your opinions with reasoned arguments and evidence.
Define	State or describe exactly the nature, extent, or meaning (of the topic).
Deliver	Actively present and engage your audience (with a concept or topic). This involves far more than simply reading from notes.
Demonstrate	Show/give lots of examples.
Describe	Give a detailed written account (of a topic).
Discuss	Examine (the topic), analyse carefully, and then present detailed considerations of advantages and disadvantages.
Evaluate	Give a reasoned judgement about the value or significance (of the topic). Give a personal appraisal, carefully identifying strengths and areas for development, advantages and limitations.
Examine	Study thoroughly to determine the nature or condition (of the topic).
Explain	Give an account of how or why (something happened), with clear reasons.
Explore	Investigate or discuss (the topic) in detail.
Identify	State or describe exactly the origin, extent, or defining characteristics (of the topic). This is similar to 'Define' above but not as in depth.
Illustrate	Make (the topic) clear by using examples, graphics, charts, etc.
Interpret	Decide what the intended meaning (of the topic) is.
Justify	Describe (what you have done/think), and give logical reasoning to support your decisions/conclusions.
List	Write a concise itemised list, using bullet points or numbering where there is a rank or sequence.
Outline	Give the main points, leaving out minor details.
Produce	Create or construct (an item, or plan, or argument).
Review	Critically assess (the topic), giving a well considered opinion.
State	Present (your topic) in a clear, brief, format.
Summarise	Give an account of the main facts in a condensed form and in your own words.

Table 6.1 Verbs used in assessment questions

Activity

Read through the assessment tasks or assessment criteria that you must evidence as part of your PTLLS Award. Identify and highlight the verbs. Now compare these with the verbs in Table 6.1 to ensure you can respond correctly.

Once you are certain of the meaning of the question and have established exactly what it requires, together with the mode of presentation and an overall word count, you can start to map the layout. For example:

- an academic essay will need to have an introduction, main content which may be separated into several sub-sections, a conclusion and a references list and/or bibliography

- a written summary may need to be divided into different sections; for example, reviewing teaching roles, responsibilities and relationships

Having mapped your assessment task into appropriate sections, allocate word counts and mini-deadlines to each.

At this stage you can start to consider relevant theories, recent developments and potential research sources such as textbooks from the recommended reading list given to you by your teacher.

Evaluation

If you are aiming to achieve at level 4, you will need to include an element of evaluation in your written work, even though this may not be obvious from the assessment question. You may need to evaluate:

- two or more methods or approaches; for example, the different approaches regarding the setting of ground rules with a group

- two or more theories; for example, contrasting the learning styles of Fleming (2005) with Honey and Mumford (1992)

- which of several items or methods is best for a purpose, stating why; for example, which assessment methods are best suited to initial, formative and summative assessment in your specialist subject area

Nearly all evaluative writing involves the processes of comparing, contrasting, critically analysing and making judgements. Your writing must always be supported by evidence from your research, that is clearly and accurately referenced.

Getting your ideas onto paper

Now you can start the process of putting your ideas onto paper. To help make sure that your content is relevant and focused, start by writing the full question to be answered at the top of the page. Read the question often as you work, continually refocusing to ensure that each point is met. Break down the question into smaller parts as it might consist of several questions which must all be addressed. You might like to highlight different stages or points of the question in bright colours, deleting or crossing out the highlights as you tackle each point.

When answering questions, make sure, if you are already teaching (in-service), that your responses are specific to the subject you are teaching, your students, the context (e.g. offender learning) and environment (e.g. workshop) within which you work. Refer to the records you use, along with relevant policies and codes of practice that you follow. If you are not yet teaching (pre-service), think about the teaching role you hope to undertake, and reflect this in your answers.

Drafting

You are now ready to start compiling your first draft. (Your final version will probably be the result of two or three subsequent drafts.) When you begin writing, start with the main body of the text. Do not attempt to write the introduction until you have completed the rest of your response. At this final stage, when you have worked right through the content, you will be in a much better position to outline and explain the way in which you have structured your response.

Write down sub-headings for each of the component parts of the question, together with any relevant examples and reference sources. The investment in developing a detailed outline at this stage will more than repay the time spent redrafting later. You can do this using hand-crafted linear notes or concept maps (see Chapter 2), or you might choose to brainstorm straight onto a computer using it to reorganise and build up your writing, stage-by-stage, into a final draft. Whichever approach you choose, restrict the first draft to recording ideas, categorising them into loose headings and identifying any links. Prioritising ideas and making corrections comes later.

Redrafting

At this second drafting stage you need to make any final adjustments to the headings in your written assessment, and write up the information you have gathered in full sentences under each of your headings. Now is also the time to check word counts against the word limits you initially allocated for each of your headings. If you are over, you will need to filter out the most important points, saving the rest for a future project. If you are under, you will need to carry out some additional work. You will need to find out if you can go over or under the word count by a certain percentage – this is usually 10 per cent.

Once you have a draft that looks sensible, you will need to read through it several times to check for sense and flow, possibly moving sections around so that the argument flows naturally between paragraphs. When you have done this, put your writing to one side, for at least a day, preferably longer: this will give you time to reflect.

Proofreading

Having left a little time between yourself and your writing, proofreading should be easier and much more effective. At this stage, it is a good idea to ask another person to look over your work for mistakes and clarity of meaning. When proofreading yourself, you should look for a smooth, logical flow between paragraphs, and examine your layout to ensure that it is consistent in terms of line spacing, use of headings, settings for right and left margins, bullet points, headers and footers, etc. References should be checked for accuracy, completeness and consistency, and you should also check your spelling, grammar and punctuation. Spelling and grammar checks built into your word-processing software can be very useful at this stage, but do not rely on them as they cannot fully account for context.

A brief outline of some key spelling, grammar and punctuation points, together with common areas of confusion follows here. For a more thorough investigation, you may wish to refer to specialist references, including the books detailed at the end of this chapter.

Spelling

If you find it hard to spell words that you have to use frequently, make an alphabetical list and keep it at hand. Try making up mnemonics (artificial aids to help memory including rhymes and acronyms).

Example

Susan has always found it difficult to spell the word 'because'. One of her peers suggested she use the mnemonic Big Elephants Can Always Understand Small Elephants (BECAUSE). She was dubious at first, but now she has found it works for her, she has started to research mnemonics for other words she finds difficult – and to create some of her own.

As well as using memory aids like mnemonics, you could identify the hard-to-spell words you use most frequently and apply a multi-sensory routine to learn them one at a time: looking at the word, saying it, covering it, writing it, saying it again and checking it. Carry out this routine two or three times a week for two or three weeks. Ongoing review is very important. You might be very pleased with the final result.

Many of the difficulties around spelling and grammar centre on nouns, verbs, adjectives, and the use of some suffixes. These are defined as follows.

noun	refers to people, animals, objects, substances, states, events and feelings; for example, *teacher, book*
verb	refers to an action (*to study, to write,* etc.) or a state (*to be, to like,* etc.); for example, to *review* your role as a teacher
adjective (modifies a noun)	describes the quality, state or action that the noun refers to; for example, the *big blue dictionary*
suffix	a letter or letters added to the end of a word to change its use or meaning, for example, help*ful*

Spellings which are a frequent cause of confusion in PTLLS assessments include the following.

- *advice* and *advise, licence* and *license, practice* and *practise* – especially when referring to the licence to practise. The rule here is that *c* is the noun and *s* is the verb – it may be easier to remember that *ice* is a noun.

- *dependant* or *dependent*. Passing the PTLLS Award is *dependent* (*adjective*) upon submitting a satisfactory portfolio. *Dependant* is the noun.

- *effect* and *affect* – *the changes in timing of the session had an effect* (*noun*) *on students' attendance, but the changes affected* (*verb*) *the students.*

- *principal* or *principle*. The *principal* (*noun*) of the college is committed to the *principle* (*noun*: belief or rule) of sustainable development and insists this should continue to be a *principal* (*adjective*: main) focus.

- use of *suffix ise* or *ize* is also problematic. Some *verbs* are never spelt with *ize*, including *advertise, advise, arise, comprise, devise, exercise* and *revise*. Other words including *organise/organize* can use either, but always be consistent.

- Another set of words that need careful checking are *homophones*: words with different meanings and spellings, but the same pronunciation. Without care, the use of *there* (it's over *there*), *they're* (they are) and *their* (belonging to them) can become muddled, and this is something that the computerised spelling checker cannot help with.

Do be careful that you are using the British English rather than the American English spellchecker.

Grammar

Grammar is the study of the structure of language. A few useful grammar points are listed here.

- Names of the days of the week and the months of the year are capitalised, but names of the seasons are not.

- Names of languages always start with a capital letter, but the names of subjects (other than languages) do not.

- Words with a direct connection to a place are capitalised (*Italian* architecture), and also those referring to nationalities (*Italian*) or ethnic groups, but their incidental use (*italian* salad dressing) is not.

- Titles of books, plays, etc., are usually in *title case*, where the first and every significant word is capitalised. However, when creating your references list, you may use title case or capitalise only the first word of the title. Whichever you choose, be consistent.

- The first word of a sentence should always start with a capital letter.

Sentences in formal writing must always be grammatically complete, i.e. express a complete idea, make sense on their own and use at least a verb and a subject, although usually sentences in English also contain an object.

Subject	Verb	Object
The teacher	prepares	the scheme of work

Be careful to ensure that your sentences are not too long by reading your work out aloud when proofreading. If you need to take a breath in the middle of a sentence, it probably needs to be divided into two (or more) shorter ones. Asking a friend or your mentor to read your work will gain another perspective.

Paragraphs, which are groups of at least three sentences of roughly similar length, should add information, explanation and clarification to a single idea until it is fully developed. Each paragraph should start with a topic sentence giving the main idea, continue with supporting sentences including description, discussion and analysis, to develop the idea, and end with a concluding sentence.

Syntax, another grammatical term, is concerned with word order in sentences and agreement in the relationship between words; for example, between subjects and verbs. Make sure that where you have a singular subject, you use a singular verb; for example, 'The teacher *models* good practice'. Similarly, a plural subject needs a plural verb, as do two singular subjects together: 'The teacher and the student *work* together'.

Tense

Assessments should normally be written in the present tense, and you should also use this tense when discussing an author's work, even if it was carried out in the past.

Example

Knowles (1990) proposes that adult learners need to understand and accept the reasons for their learning.

However, biographical information about an author should be in the past tense.

Example

Knowles, who was born in 1913, was a leading academic in principles of adult education.

When talking about your own practice, ideas and opinions, you should write in the first person singular; otherwise you should use the third person, but never the second. Writing in the first person demonstrates your understanding and shows how you would put theory into practice. For example,

'I would establish ground rules with my students by...' is correct; you would not write 'you would establish ground rules with your students by...' or 'he would establish ground rules with his students by...' as you are not talking about someone else. You need to claim ownership of your actions and writing in the first person does this.

	Singular	Plural
First person	I	we
Second person	you	you
Third person	he/she/it	they

You also need to distinguish between the active and the passive voice, always using the active voice in the first person. A sentence is said to be in the active voice if the subject performs an action (the subject being the person).

Example

First person active: **I completed an excellent assignment.**

Third person active: **The student completed an excellent assignment.**

Third person passive: **An excellent assignment was completed by the student.**

Some awarding organisations require aspects of written assessments to be written in the third person passive. For example, *the scheme of work was prepared by the teacher* (third person passive) rather than *the teacher prepared the scheme of work* (third person active).

Punctuation

Punctuation is a system of using marks or characters within writing, to separate aspects of it, to make the meaning of a sentence clear.

The first four punctuation marks discussed can be thought of as units of pause, where a comma is one unit, a semi-colon two units, a colon two-and-a-half or three units, and a full stop is four (West, 2008).

Commas are used to mark off parts of a sentence to make meaning clearer, and they have four basic uses.

- Linking two sentences with a conjunction; for example, *or*, *but*, *while* and *yet*.

- Adding extra information. Information added at the start or end of a sentence requires only one comma. Information added in the middle needs to be bracketed by a comma at either end.

- Separating items in a list.

- Segmenting large numbers.

Semi-colons are used to:

- link together two sentences which are closely related or reflect each other; for example, *Abbas was pleased; he had completed his PTLLS Award*

- separate listed items which are particularly long or have commas within them; for example, ... *the blurb, a short promotional description usually on the back page; the abstract, if there is one; ... references list; and bibliography*

Colons are used to:

- separate a title and a subtitle; the year of publication from the page number in a reference in the body of the text; and the place of publication from the publishers in a reference list

- introduce a word, list, summary or quotation; whatever comes after the colon should explain, show or resolve whatever comes before: *Only one thing is likely to result from an unplanned micro-teach: referral*

A full stop should mark the end of a sentence. Using a comma instead will create an unacceptable run-on sentence or comma splice. Exclamation marks should also be avoided in formal writing. Question marks should always be used at the end of a direct question; for example, 'Is your assessment ready to hand in?' but not for reported questions; for example, *She asked him if his assessment was ready to hand in.*

Apostrophes have the following uses.

- To show missing letters.

I'm – I am	*You're* – You are	*It's* – it is or it has
I haven't – I have not	*You can't* – You cannot	*Don't* – Do not

  As the contracted form should not be used in formal writing, you will be concerned primarily with its second use.

- (a) To show that something belongs to, or is a part of, someone or something else.

Radcliffe's laptop	*The teacher's pens*	*This week's Times Ed.*
Ravi's sister	*The student's portfolio*	*Yesterday's paper*

  (The apostrophe goes after the word or name and before the s.)

  (b) To show that something belongs to, or is a part of, more than one person or thing.

The teachers' files	*The students' desks*	*Three days' work*

  (Where the plural is created by adding an s, the apostrophe follows the s.)

The children's toys	*The people's decision*	*Everyone's safety*

  (Where the word is already a plural, return to the first rule and put the apostrophe after the word, and before the s.)

- There is a different rule for *it's* and *its*.

  To mean *it is* or *it has*: *it's*

  To show something belongs to *it*: *its* (no apostrophe); for example, *its fur is soft.* This is also true of other pronouns: *ours, hers, yours.*

Apostrophes are not used when indicating more than one of something (plurals), or for decades; for example, 1900s, not 1900's.

Activity

Have a go at correcting the following.

Its important to ensure that all teachers are aware of their roles and responsibilities, especially with regard to Health and Safety. In the same way, its important for students to recognise the need for them to ensure each others and other peoples safety. Its no longer enough, since moving beyond the 1900s, simply to put a sign above equipment warning of the dangers of its misuse.

The corrected version appears below. Well done if you were able to complete the activity successfully. If not, work through the explanations again.

> *It's important to ensure that all teachers are aware of their roles and responsibilities, especially with regard to Health and Safety. In the same way, it's important for all students to recognise the need for them to ensure each other's and other people's safety. It's no longer enough, since moving beyond the 1900s, simply to put a sign above equipment warning of the dangers of its misuse.*

Brackets (parentheses) are of two different types.

- Round brackets are used to encase information that is relevant, but not essential to a sentence. They are also used to enclose the year of publication, and the date an internet site was accessed when using the Harvard referencing system (see Chapter 5).

- Square brackets are used to enter extra information into quotations to aid clarity, and, in Harvard referencing, to signify an electronic source; for example, [online].

Quotation marks should always be used to denote direct speech, or short extracts taken directly from others' writing. Single quotation marks are generally used, but for quotations inside quotations, you should use double quotation marks; for example, ... a recent report concerning accessibility of venues stated that 'over 90% of respondents were "very happy" with provision'.

Quotation marks can also be used to denote a definition or name, but increasingly italics are being used for this purpose.

An ellipsis, three evenly spaced dots (...), with one space between the ellipsis and its surrounding letters or other marks, indicates that words have been purposely left out of a quotation, generally in the interests of brevity or to highlight key points.

Hyphens are often used for clarity when connecting two words; for example, *re-word, re-focus, twenty-one*. The hyphen is a shorter mark than the dash and has no spaces on either side.

The dash – which can be used for explanation, emphasis, or in the place of brackets or commas – is longer than the hyphen and has spaces on both sides.

Top tip: with any of these points above, if you are unsure, find out or reword your text to avoid the problem.

Using pictures, charts, etc., to support your writing

Information can be communicated in a variety of ways. Pictures, charts, graphs, diagrams and symbols can all be used to add clarification and interest to your written assessments. Whenever you use such an illustration, however, you should take care to ensure that it is clearly labelled and supports or explains the text, or that text is included to describe the illustration.

Charts and graphs must always be carefully and accurately constructed, using a chart type and scale or scales that enable the most effective display of the data. Generally, you should place the dependent variable on the y axis and the independent variable on the x axis.

For example, as monthly college attendance figures (dependent variable) depend upon the months of the academic year (independent variable), the attendance figures would be shown on the y axis in a two-dimensional (2D) representation (with an additional z axis the graph is a 3D representation), and the months of the year on the x axis. See Figure 6.1.

			In the example (Figure 4.1) below
y axis (z axis 3D)	vertical axis	dependent variable	Number of students
x axis	horizontal axis	independent variable	Months

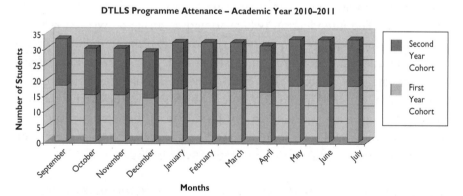

Figure 6.1 Column chart

You will need to give a title to the chart or graph and to the axes, as in Figure 6.1, and always include the units of measurement. The title appears above the chart or graph, whereas with figures it always appears below. If you have more than one set of data, show each series using a different colour or symbol and include clear labels. Effective graphs, charts and diagrams can be constructed using word processing or spreadsheet software and either cut and pasted or linked into your assessment tasks.

When using any illustrations or figures created by others, always check any copyright limitations and accurately acknowledge your sources when referencing.

Formal writing

Your written assessment tasks will need to be presented in a formal written style, following set procedures for structure and presentation.

General guidance for the structure of work

As you start to write more, particularly if you progress from the PTLLS Award to a higher-level teaching qualification, you will start to develop your own style. Perusing books and newspapers that you enjoy can help you to develop your knowledge of paragraphing, sentence construction and punctuation. Reading widely can also help your spelling and grammar. If you see words that don't look correct, it could be that you have always spelt them wrong but were not aware of it.

It is important that your written assessments are soundly structured with a logical flow. The introduction (which should normally be written last after you have addressed the requirements) should explain your interpretation of the question and how you have structured your answer in response, outlining the key content. The main content should then build on the introduction, and lead into a conclusion which should summarise the main points of your writing, picking up on the theme of the introduction. If you are aiming for level 4, you should extend your conclusion to suggest wider implications and maybe predict future trends or issues.

General guidance for the presentation of written assessments

Written assessments should be presented using a standard layout, giving consistency throughout all work submitted for your portfolio. You should always check with your teacher/assessor for any specific presentation requirements of the PTLLS Award.

Title

The title, usually in the form of the question to be answered, should be set out in full at the top of the first page.

Layout

As far as possible, all work should be word-processed in double- or one-and-a-half-line spacing. Use a standard font, which is easy to read (Arial or Verdana are good choices), usually in size 12 point. Allow a left-hand margin of at least 30mm to accommodate hole-punching or other binding.

Referencing

Harvard referencing should normally be used (see Chapter 5). Referencing your work is essential if you are aiming for level 4. If you are aiming for level 3, it is good practice to include a bibliography, although you must include a references list if you cite or quote other authors in your writing.

Word counts

Where you are given a word count, it is important to keep within this, and to state the number of words at the beginning or end of your writing. If you are given a word range; for example, 350–500 words, your assessment should be inside the range. Where you are given a simple count; for example, 500 words, you are generally allowed 10 per cent either side; for example, 450–550 words.

Identity

All your work should be identifiable. Make sure that you put your name and/or enrolment number on every page, and, as far as is practicable, on every piece of accompanying material, such as resources used for your micro-teach. It is most effective to include this in a header or footer, so that it will automatically appear at the same place on every page of a document, no matter how many times you add or remove content. The date of submission could also be added within the header or footer.

Page numbering

Your pages should always be consecutively numbered, preferably using the automatic page numbering facility; for example, 'page *x* of *y*'. This facility will automatically count the pages in each document and display the current page number relative to the total number of pages.

General guidance for compiling your PTLLS portfolio

Declaration of authenticity

You will be asked to sign a document confirming that the evidence you submit is authentic and a true representation of your own work. This is to help guard against plagiarism (the use of someone else's work without proper acknowledgement). For more details, see Chapter 5.

Anonymity of students

If you are currently teaching and using examples from your teaching practice to contextualise your assessment tasks, be careful to keep students' personal data confidential. If you do need to name students, either use an identification system such as *Student A*, *Student B*, etc., or give your students pseudonyms (or aliases). Where you choose the latter, make this clear by including a statement such as 'In the interests of confidentiality, all student names used are pseudonyms'.

Safe-keeping

Any work submitted should always be securely fastened and you should always keep copies. It is rare for work to go astray, but if something goes missing, you will need to resubmit it. If you have to post assessments, sending them by Special Delivery Next Day or Recorded Signed For will enable you to track their delivery. All work produced on a computer should be backed up to an alternative storage device, such as an external USB (universal serial bus) hard drive, USB flash drive (or memory stick), memory card (e.g. SD, micro SD, Compact Flash), DVD or CD. You can also use cloud computing solutions where your information is held on line, and therefore has the added advantage that it can be accessed from any computer, subject of course to a working internet connection. Examples of cloud storage include Dropbox, SkyDrive, SugarSync, TeamDrive and ZumoDrive. Another useful trick, if you have an available internet connection, is to email yourself an attachment of your work.

Extenuating circumstances

Note the deadlines for all assessment tasks and keep them to hand, checking your progress regularly. You will be expected to plan your study so that you can meet assessment deadlines around work, family and other commitments. If you do find that you need an extension owing to extenuating circumstances, discuss this with your teacher/assessor as soon as possible.

General guidance for the final presentation of your PTLLS portfolio

It is a good idea to ask your teacher about the presentation of your portfolio early on in the PTLLS Award programme, so that you can compile it as you go. This helps keep your work safe and reduces the amount of searching and sorting needed to get everything together at the end. If you are producing a conventional paper-based portfolio, you will need to make sure your portfolio binder or folder is clearly labelled, on the front cover and the spine, with your name, programme title, and programme code (if applicable). Every page submitted should be immediately visible. It is straightforward to hole-punch each sheet of paper, putting these directly into your file (remember to allow sufficiently wide margins – at least 2.54cm either side – so as not to punch holes through your text). If you choose instead to use plastic pockets, you will need one for every two sides of content. Always ask first about this, as some organisations do not allow these.

Instead of using a paper-based portfolio, you might be expected to use an electronic- or e-portfolio. E-portfolios are very similar to typical paper-based portfolios, in that they hold the evidence you provide but, as well as conventional media, they also enable the inclusion of a wider range of evidence types, such as digital pictures, audio excerpts and video recordings.

There are several dedicated e-portfolio systems currently available, such as Learning Assistant, OneFile, Pebblepad, Quickstep and SmartAssessor, as well as Virtual Learning Environments (VLEs), such as Blackboard, Bodington, Moodle or Wimba, which can perform the dual functions of being a teaching and learning environment and e-portfolio.

The benefits of e-portfolios are:

● information is held centrally, is accessible at any time, not only by you, but also by your assessor. This often means that you can get feedback on your assignments more quickly than if you had to wait for face-to-face meetings

● you can use hyperlinks to make connections between different sections of your portfolio. This makes it much easier and quicker to link one piece of evidence to several assessment criteria

- an e-portfolio can be easily duplicated and adapted for different purposes

- many e-portfolio systems include an easy-to-use visual tracking system. You can see at a glance what evidence you have submitted and completed, and what is still left to do. Many students find this highly motivating.

- there are no heavy folders for you to carry around as everything is kept online

- you can save on stationery costs

- once uploaded, your work should be regularly backed-up to a central storage point, reducing the likelihood of loss or damage

Disadvantages include:

- the need for ready access to IT facilities and internet access on an ongoing basis

- the need for appropriate IT skills and training in how to use the e-portfolio

- learning providers often restrict the time you are able to access your e-portfolio after you have finished your qualification, so you may need to keep your own electronic copies of evidence submitted if you want them to be available in the long term. This is something you need to ask your teacher about at the beginning of your course, as it is much easier to make copies as you go along, rather than trying to retrieve everything at the end

Whatever format you are using, all evidence should be clearly cross-referenced to the assessment criteria. It is good practice to include a contents list. Besides being assessed, your portfolio may be sampled by an internal quality assurer and/or an external quality assurer on behalf of the Awarding Organisation. They will not want to waste time searching through an unorganised file to find what they need.

Presenting your work in practice

Preparing for your micro-teach

Part of your practical assessment for your PTLLS Award will be to deliver a short micro-teach session either to your peers, or possibly if you are already teaching, to students at your normal place of work. The micro-teach will be for a minimum of 15 minutes, and will be observed by your teacher/ assessor. Micro-teaching is a scaled-down teaching and learning experience designed to help develop new teaching skills and provide opportunities to polish and perfect existing ones. You will have an opportunity to put theory into practice, obtain feedback from your teacher and possibly your peers, as well as to undertake a reflective self-evaluation.

There are many benefits of an observed micro-teach; for example, you will be able to:

- build self-confidence

- experiment in a safe environment

- identify the positive qualities of others

- develop processes of self-evaluation

- give and receive feedback

- have your good practice recognised and supported

- start to develop a personal teaching style

When preparing for your micro-teach, the delivery time may seem like an eternity. In reality, it is very little time, and you will need to plan your timings extremely carefully to make sure that you deliver a meaningful session to your peers or students. Your delivery should consist of an introduction, development and summary. The latter should include revisiting your aim and objectives and time for student questions.

When delivering your micro-teach you should plan to:

- enable the group to learn a basic concept
- demonstrate how to write clear and effective objectives or learning outcomes
- select suitable teaching and learning approaches, and use resources effectively
- carry out appropriate assessment

Make sure that you obtain a copy of your assessor's observation checklist well in advance of your micro-teach session, so that you know exactly what they will be looking for.

You will need to write your session plan and prepare resources, including presentation slides and printed learning materials, in advance. It is important to make these as accessible as possible. For example, with handouts you should restrict the amount of text on the page, leaving spaces between columns and including wide margins and spaces between paragraphs. Headings and new sections should come at the top of pages wherever possible, and sentences and paragraphs should be kept within columns or pages. Use a clear font; for example, Arial, Comic Sans or Verdana, with a minimum font size of 12 point, and a maximum of 14 point. Number your pages clearly. If you have students with any special requirements it's advisable to ask them if they would prefer learning materials with a different coloured background, or a particular font and size.

Readability

Readability is an attempt to match the reading level of written material to the reading with understanding level of the reader. For maximum readability, use short sentences (see Chapter 6) including only one main point, and ending with a full stop. Use the active voice, and where possible, simple, straightforward words. If you have to use technical terms, explain them first. There are several readability tests to assess density of writing. The quickest and easiest to use manually is the SMOG (Simplified Measure of Gobbledygook) readability formula, which calculates readability using sentence and word length.

Activity

Obtain a textbook or a newspaper and carry out a SMOG test using the SMOG calculator in Appendix 4. You might like to use a textbook in your subject area to see how relevant it would be for your own students.

If you want a text to be readily understood by the majority of people, it should be at a readability level of 10 or below.

The following should apply to all printed learning materials, writing on whiteboards, and presentation slides that you wish to use.

• Use a combination of upper and lower case letters as the shapes of the words helps word recognition. If you use only capital letters it appears as though you are shouting.

• Embolden text or surround it with a box for emphasis, and avoid positioning text at unusual angles.

- Use a ragged right margin. Justifying the right-hand margin distorts letter spacing and can give the appearance of rivers of white space running down the page.

- Wherever you use illustrations, make sure that these are in context and support the text, or they are likely to confuse.

- Proofread all your work carefully to eliminate errors.

- Reference any text from sources.

When it comes to the day of the micro-teach, do not worry if you feel tense: it is okay to feel nervous. You could try using some relaxation techniques.

Example

Today is the day of Simon's micro-teach. He listens to his favourite music on his journey to the venue, and finds that he arrives in a reasonably relaxed state. As the time for him to start draws near, he shrugs his shoulders and tenses and releases his body gently while sitting in his chair. Immediately before starting, he leaves the room for two minutes, and standing outside, breathes deeply from his diaphragm. As he enters the room to start his session, he takes one deep breath, stands tall, and remembers to speak a little more slowly than usual. These preparations enable him to start his micro-teach in a reasonably relaxed state, and he is soon at ease as he falls into the rhythm of his presentation.

On the day, you will probably find that the time will simply fly past. Remember to position a clock where you can check it discreetly, and to note down your start and finishing time somewhere equally accessible.

For more detailed information about aspects of micro-teaching, please see Chapter 13 of *Passing PTLLS Assessments* by Ann Gravells.

Effective presentations

Being able to present information in an interesting and accessible manner is a key teaching skill that has to be learned and practised.

Delivering an effective presentation

One of the best ways to establish what something looks like when it works well is to isolate what happens when it does not.

Activity

Spend ten minutes identifying what you consider are the ten major mistakes made by presenters. Reflect on presentations that you have attended, or that you might have delivered yourself. Think about what happened from the start of the presentation, through to the finish. Make a note of your thoughts on a separate sheet of paper.

How many did you manage to come up with? The ten major mistakes made by presenters identified by Malouf (1997) are:

1. failing to speak to time

2. using material unsuited to the audience

3. information overload

4. material that is too technical

5. poor preparation

6. failure to practise speech

7. distracting visuals/verbals/vocals

8. inappropriate pace

9. lack of eye contact

10. lack of enthusiasm

These same mistakes also often occur in micro-teaches; after all, a substantial part of your micro-teach involves presenting to your audience of students. You can adopt some of the following strategies to help make sure that these things do not happen to you.

Rehearse, rehearse, rehearse

Perfect preparation prevents poor performance. There is no substitute for planning and practising your micro-teach thoroughly, timing it as you do so. It is important to note, however, that your perfected rehearsal with a small, or even no, audience is likely to proceed much more quickly than the real thing. Always have an exercise that can be left out without detriment, or included to add value, depending upon how the time goes.

Prepare for set-up issues

Arrive at least 15–20 minutes early to set everything up, and carry out a check for any health and safety issues. Make sure you have a contingency plan available in case of last-minute equipment failures, etc.

Enthusiasm is contagious

It is difficult for your audience not to enjoy and engage with your presentation if you are delivering it with passion and enthusiasm. Furthermore, any nerves will abate when you are excited about your subject matter.

Speak to your students

Reading from a script can cause you to lose eye contact with your group. Your voice projection will also be reduced as you look downwards into your paper. If you do want to use notes for support, write out key words or phrases onto a set of plain postcards (which should be numbered and treasury-tagged together so that they stay in order if you should drop them), or use an electronic slide presentation as a prompt.

Involve your students

Be careful to engage with your audience. Find out about any prior knowledge that anyone might have, so that you can build on this throughout your session. Use your students' names, and be careful to involve and ask questions to everyone. Observe your students' reactions and try to keep up an appropriate pace.

Choose your material carefully

Remember your audience when designing your material. Make sure it is pitched at the right level and not excessively technical. Avoid the use of jargon, and explain technical words where they are necessary. Keep your content simple. You do not have a great deal of time.

Maximise eye contact and visibility

Be careful not to block your presentation material by walking or standing in front of your screen, whiteboard or flipchart. If you have an electronic presentation, using a remote mouse will allow you to advance slides without always being close to the computer. If you use the whiteboard, remember not to talk while writing with your back to your students, to enable everyone to see and hear you.

Minimise distraction

When you decide on your outfit, avoid loose clothing, pockets or jewellery that might encourage you to fidget, and make sure you feel comfortable. Try not to overuse words or fillers such as *you know* or *erm*. Turn off, or put away from view, equipment such as digital projectors or props when you are not using them. If you are using Microsoft PowerPoint, pressing the *b* key on the keyboard will blank out the screen, and pressing it a second time will bring it back.

Designing an effective slide presentation

There are many advantages to using presentation software to support your micro-teach. Well-prepared slides including images can offer invaluable support to visual students. The slides can also act as a focus for you, with your key information logically and sequentially ordered. The use of ICT will also help to demonstrate your application of this part of the minimum core. When using presentation software, the following will help to ensure an effective and trouble-free presentation.

Choose an appropriate slide design

Choose a simple slide background that offers good visibility. A dark blue background with yellow text is generally accessible to the greatest number of people. Some of the animation features can be used to good effect, such as bringing in bullet points one at a time, but use them sparingly.

Use clear text supported by appropriate pictures and charts

Titles should be in a font size between 32 and 50 point, with all other text between 24 and 32 point. A font such as Arial or Verdana is easy to read. Each slide should have no more than six to eight bullet points, showing key phrases. You should talk through your slides, explaining each item in complete sentences and giving examples. Use the slides purely for confirmation and emphasis. Use pictures and charts where they can help to clarify the text.

Test your presentation beforehand

It is always a good idea to test your presentation on the equipment you will be using prior to the teaching session itself. Issues of compatibility can arise with different hardware and different makes and versions of software.

Information communication technology

Being able to work effectively with ICT, whatever your subject specialism, is an important teaching skill, and ICT, together with literacy, language and numeracy, is now part of the required minimum core of teachers' knowledge, understanding and personal skills. As well as being able to use presentation software, you will usually be required to word-process your PTLLS assessments, and to use the internet and other electronic media such as e-books, CDs and DVDs, podcasts and online videos for research. If you are undertaking a blended or online learning programme, you will also need to find your way around the VLE (virtual learning environment).

If you do not have access to a commercial word processing and presentation package, you could download OpenOffice (http://download.openoffice. org), which is a free package of programs compatible with many Microsoft documents.

Activity

Follow the link to the Open Office templates page at http://templates. services.openoffice.org/en/node/3247 **and look through the lists of templates that can be downloaded. Examine in more detail any you think could be useful.**

Specific information communication skills you will need

In order to produce assessments for your PTLLS Award, as a minimum you should be able to:

- create a new document
- save a document to your computer hard drive and to a USB flash drive
- open an existing document
- input text

- use the cut, copy and paste facilities

- change margins

- change font size and style

- alter line-spacing – there is a simple automatic function to change line spacing anywhere in a document

- create and use headers and footers

- use automatic page numbering

- use automatic bullets and numbering

- create tables and sort the contents alphabetically

- use the search and replace facility

- use the automatic word count facility.

Due to the different software suppliers and different software versions, it is not possible to give information on how to perform these functions. You may, however, find some online resources helpful.

- *Go on, make online easy* at http://learn.go-on.co.uk/. This is a government website designed to help people take their first steps with computers and the internet. Users get access to an easy-to-use email system and a wide range of online courses.

- *Digital Unite Learning Zone* at http://learning.digitalunite.com. Digital Unite is an independent organisation established in 1996, whose Learning Zone contains a wide variety of free online guides designed to support users, from the complete beginner to the more experienced, in making the most of digital technology.

Summary

In this chapter you have learned about:

- Presenting your work in writing

  – deciding on a structure

  – getting your ideas onto paper

  – using pictures, charts, etc., to support your writing

  – formal writing

- Presenting your work in practice

  - preparing for your micro-teach

  - effective presentations

  - information communication technology

Theory focus

Books

Crystal, D. (2004) *Rediscover grammar*, (3rd Edn.) Harlow: Pearson Education.

Fleming, N. (2005) *Teaching and learning styles: VARK strategies*. Honolulu: Honolulu Community College.

Gravells, A. (2012a) *Preparing to Teach in the Lifelong Learning Sector*, (5th Edn.) London: Learning Matters.

Gravells, A. (2012b) *Passing PTLLS Assessments*, (2nd Edn.) London: Learning Matters.

Honey, P. and Mumford, A. (1992) *The manual of learning styles*, (3rd Edn.) Maidenhead: Peter Honey Associates.

Knowles, M. (1990) *The adult student: a neglected species*, (4th Edn.) Houston: Gulf Publishing.

Malouf, D. (1997) *How to create and deliver a dynamic presentation*. USA: ASTD Press.

Petty, G. (2009) *Evidence based teaching*, (2nd Edn.) Cheltenham: Nelson Thornes.

Rogers, C. (1980) *Freedom to learn for the 80s*. New York: Free Press.

Truss, L. (2003) *Eats, shoots and leaves*. London: Profile Books Limited.

Watson, J. (1924) *Behaviourism*. New York: Norton.

West, C. (2008) *Perfect written English*. London: Random House Books.

Websites

ArmoredPenguin (word puzzles)	www.armoredpenguin.com
Digital Unite Learning Zone	http://learning.digitalunite.com
Go on, make online easy	http://learn.go-on.co.uk
Microsoft Digital Literacy Curriculum	www.microsoft.com/uk/education/ schools/curriculum-resources/digital-literacy-curriculum.aspx
Open Office	http://download.openoffice.org http://templates.services.openoffice. org/en/node/3247
Royal Mail Group Limited – postage	www.royalmail.com
SMOG	www.literacytrust.org.uk/campaign/ SMOG.html

Introduction

In this chapter you will learn about:

- transferable skills
- teaching in the Lifelong Learning Sector
- lifelong learning

There are activities and examples to help you reflect on the above which will assist your understanding of how to move forward after achieving your PTLLS Award.

Transferable skills

Transferable skills are skills and attributes developed in one context, in this case studying for your PTLLS Award, which can be transferred to other areas of your work and life. Examples of transferable skills include:

- decision-making
- information communication technology (ICT) skills
- numeracy
- organisation and planning
- presentation skills
- problem-solving
- self-direction and motivation
- spoken and written communication skills
- team-working
- time management

Activity

Spend 15 minutes reviewing and listing the skills you have developed while studying for the PTLLS Award. Refer back to the activities on learning styles and expert student characteristics in Chapter 1, and the study skills and learning goals activities in Chapter 2. Revisit your reflective learning journal and your portfolio of evidence to remind you of work completed and distance travelled. Consider how you can apply these skills in different areas of your life; for example, other employment, hobbies and interests, or in the home.

It is useful to carry out a personal SWOT analysis (**S**trengths, **W**eaknesses, **O**pportunities, **T**hreats) at regular intervals to identify internal and exter-nal factors impacting on you and your continuing professional development (CPD). As well as providing a focus for specific professional development planning (PDP), this will help to highlight additional transferable skills that would enable you to perform more effectively in all areas of your life.

Example

Having successfully completed his PTLLS Award, Tariq starts work on a SWOT analysis as a focus for his future PDP. He uses the term areas for development, *rather than weaknesses. Here are his initial entries.*

Strengths	Areas for development
PTLLS Award at level 3	Achieve CTLLS
Fluent French and Arabic speaker	Improve English spelling and grammar
Excellent ICT skills – ITQ3	Work on inter-personal and team-working skills
Confident in, and good at, maths	Pass driving test
Self-motivated and enthusiastic	
Opportunities	**Threats**
CTLLS course starting in two months' time	College restructuring – redundancies
Volunteer teaching role at community centre	Too few teaching practice hours
Free English grammar course at local centre	Dependent on public transport

Once you have completed a SWOT analysis, you can use it to identify short-, medium- and long-term SMART (**S**pecific, **M**easurable, **A**chievable, **R**ealistic, **T**ime-bound) development goals. You should monitor these regularly, updating them when:

- your personal or professional circumstances change

- new technology emerges that affects your subject specialism and/or teaching skills

- organisational and wider developments impact on your job role

Teaching in the Lifelong Learning Sector

From the date of your appointment in a teaching role in the Lifelong Learning Sector, you have five years to gain your Licence to Practise. This is through achievement of the relevant qualification, a process of professional formation and an ongoing commitment to CPD.

This book was written prior to the Lord Lingfield Interim Report *Professionalism in Further Education* (2012). There may have been some changes to the requirements for teachers in the Lifelong Learning Sector as a result of the subsequent report which was due after this book was published.

Following achievement of your PTLLS Award, the next steps towards gaining your Licensed Practitioner Status are to:

- ensure you are registered with the Institute for Learning (IfL)

- work out the date by which you need to achieve Licensed Practitioner Status

- take steps to ensure your subject specialist knowledge is, and continues to be, current and sufficient

- make the necessary arrangements to obtain the teaching practice needed

- enrol on an appropriate teaching qualification course; for example, CTLLS for Associate Teachers (ATLS), or DTLLS/Certificate in Education/PGCE for Qualified Teachers (QTLS)

- consider how you will meet the requirements for the Minimum Core in ICT, literacy, language, numeracy and ICT, if you do not already have the evidence needed

Activity

Follow the link, www.move-on.org.uk/practicetests.asp, to access the Move-on website where you can find a selection of literacy and numeracy National Test practice papers and resources. The National Tests at level 2 could be used to evidence literacy and numeracy skills for professional formation. Register on the site and explore some of the practice papers or hot topics.

You can obtain details regarding the minimum core at http://www.lluk. org/3043.htm which also includes ICT. Improving your own skills in these areas will also help your students' skills.

Professional status

To gain professional status of ATLS or QTLS, following achievement of CTLLS or DTLLS, you will need to complete a period of professional formation. This is when you show, over a period of time, that you can apply your skills and knowledge effectively and meet the LLUK overarching professional teaching standards. These standards, which identify what teachers should know and be able to do, are divided into six domains.

A Professional values and practice.

B Learning and teaching.

C Specialist learning and teaching.

D Planning for learning.

E Assessment for learning.

F Access and progression. (LLUK, 2006)

Timetable

From the date of appointment, all new teachers must:

- register with the IfL within 6 months
- complete the PTLLS Award within 12 months
- complete CTLLS or DTLLS/Certificate in Education/PGCE and achieve ATLS or QTLS status within five years
- demonstrate ongoing commitment to CPD

Professional formation

Professional formation is the process undertaken after achieving CTLLS, DTLLS or the equivalent qualifications. It enables you to gain ATLS or QTLS status by demonstrating through professional practice:

- the ability to make effective use of the skills and knowledge gained during training
- the capacity to meet the national occupational teaching standards

The full process entails completing and submitting an expression of intent through the members' area of the IfL website, before providing evidence of:

- achievement of an approved teaching qualification at level 5 or above for QTLS, and level 3 or 4 for ATLS
- achievement of numeracy and literacy skills at level 2 or above
- current teaching and learning
- subject specialist knowledge and currency
- self-evaluation
- developmental planning
- reflective practice
- a supporting testimony

The evidence you provide will include scanned copies of qualifications, written statements and a declaration of suitability, made against IfL criteria. All your evidence should be submitted via the IfLs REfLECT webpage.

Continuing professional development (CPD)

Full-time teachers in the further education sector are required to under-take, document and reflect on at least 30 hours of CPD per year, reduced pro-rata for part-time staff (subject to a minimum of six hours). CPD includes any activity undertaken for the purposes of updating specialist subject knowledge or developing teaching skills (OPSI, 2007).

Opportunities for continuing professional development include:

- attending events and courses
- improving own skills such as ICT

- shadowing colleagues

- researching developments or changes to your subject and/or relevant legislation

- self-reflecting

- study for relevant qualifications

- reading relevant journals

- relevant voluntary work

Any method can be used to plan and document CPD, but as part of the services they offer, the IfL provide REfLECT, a dedicated and secure online personal learning space where members are able to plan, record and assess the impact of CPD on their practice (www.ifl.ac.uk/cpd/reflect). You can then self-declare completion of your CPD by completing a form on the IfL website. If you do not want to use their website, you can maintain your records manually or electronically in another form. If your CPD record is selected as part of the IfL sampling process, you will be asked to provide all your details. Results from this sample will form part of the IfL annual report.

Code of Professional Practice

All members of the IfL agree to be bound by their Code of Professional Practice, which came into effect on 1 April 2008. This code outlines the *Behaviours* expected of members for the benefit of students, the profession, employers and the wider community:

- Behaviour 1: Professional Integrity

- Behaviour 2: Respect

- Behaviour 3: Reasonable Care

- Behaviour 4: Professional Practice

- Behaviour 5: Criminal Offence Disclosure

- Behaviour 6: Responsibility during Institute Investigations

- Behaviour 7: Responsibility to the Institute

The code will be subject to regular review to ensure that it remains relevant and reflects advances in professional practice. Full details can be accessed at www.ifl.ac.uk/professional-standards/code-of-professional-practice

Lifelong learning

New professional standards for teachers, tutors and trainers in the Lifelong Learning Sector were published in January 2007 by Lifelong Learning UK (LLUK) as part of extensive government reforms in England to improve professionalisation and performance standards in the lifelong learning workforce. They set out agreed standards for professional performance, as the basis for new generic teaching qualifications (including the PTLLS Award), subject qualifications for teaching literacy, numeracy and ESOL, and continuing professional development (CPD) in the sector. New qualification guidance has also been developed in 2011 for teaching disabled learners.

Separate, but related, Professional Standards exist for teachers in each of the four nations. A guide for using these new professional standards in England was published by LLUK in March 2011 and is available from www. excellencegateway.org.uk/page.aspx?o=320923. Please see the web links at the end of this chapter for Northern Ireland, Scotland and Wales.

LLUK was, in 2007, one of 25 UK Sector Skills Councils and was responsible for the professional development of staff working in the Lifelong Learning Sector. As part of this role, it was responsible for developing the qualifications and setting standards for the delivery and support of learning. LLUK reviewed all teaching qualifications between October 2010 and March 2011.

It viewed lifelong learning as *a catalyst for a better society* defining it as learning that happens outside a school environment (LLUK, 2009: 15).

It suggested lifelong learning could include:

> ... *learning new work skills or updating existing skills as job requirements change. Or it might be the inspiration people find at a youth group, or the opportunity for learning at a local library*
>
> (LLUK, 2009:17).

Lifelong learning, therefore, can be any learning undertaken at any age and at any time.

According to Microsoft (2008):

- many learners who started a three-year degree in 2010 are likely to find half of their first year's learning obsolete by the end of their studies

- there are about five times as many words in the English language now as during Shakespeare's time

- one week's issues of *The Times* probably contain more information than an average person saw in an eighteenth-century lifetime

The rate and scale of change engulfing the world is creating a tidal shift in how people live and earn their living (Robinson, 2011).

Together these insights provide the cornerstone of a clear rationale for lifelong learning, demonstrating its essential nature for both individuals and society, not now to advance, but simply not to fall behind.

Organisations involved in the teaching reforms

Learning and Skills Improvement Service (LSIS)

As part of a new government structure, since 1 April 2011 the Learning and Skills Improvement Service (LSIS) took over responsibility for Further Education in England (including work-based learning and adult and community learning).

LSIS is the sector-owned body that is charged with delivering high-quality improvement and strategic change in the learning and skills sector, enhancing professionalism for the lifelong learning workforce across the nations and regions of the UK.

The Standards and Qualifications team is a part of the wider LSIS UK Qualifications and Skills team (UKQST) who act as a link between employers, professionals, partners and policy makers, and work on the development of national occupational standards, qualifications and apprenticeship frameworks.

LSIS is currently producing an up-to-date guide for teaching in the Further Education (FE) sector, including information about the current qualifications and how they will change as a result of the 2010–2011 LLUK review. This is to be published on their website (www.lsis.org.uk) in April 2012.

Institute for Learning (IfL)

The Institute for Learning (IfL) is the professional body for teachers, trainers and assessors in the learning and skills sector. It is led by members for members and embraces adult and community learning, emergency and public services, FE colleges, the armed services, the voluntary sector and work-based learning (IfL, 2009). It remains responsible for learner registration and provision of the award of licensed practitioner status: Qualified Teacher Learning and Skills (QTLS) for full teaching roles, or Associate

Teacher Learning and Skills (ATLS) for associate teacher roles. In addition, it has taken on responsibility for three areas of work previously carried out by Standards Verification UK (SVUK), a former subsidiary of LLUK.

1. Quality assuring and endorsing the qualifications put forward by LSIS, including the maintenance of a register of approved teaching qualification for further education and skills. An Awarding Organisation, for example City & Guilds, will then produce a syllabus based upon the national occupational standards.

2. Managing the process for mapping legacy qualifications and teaching and training qualifications awarded by bodies outside the further education and skills sector in England, to the national standards. This includes the transfer and ongoing development of the Tariff of Qualifications previously hosted by SVUK.

3. Supporting candidates in the final stages of SVUK's General Professional Recognition Learning and Skills (GPRLS) scheme, ensuring that those who began GPRLS are not disadvantaged by the closure of LLUK and SVUK and have the opportunity to have their knowledge and expertise recognised. IfL has committed to explore an alternative to GPRLS through the creation of an experiential route to the full professional status of Qualified Teacher Learning and Skills (QTLS).

Summary

In this chapter you have learned about:

- transferable skills
- teaching in the Lifelong Learning Sector
- lifelong learning

Theory focus

Books

Gravells, A. (2012a) *Preparing to Teach in the Lifelong Learning Sector*, (5th Edn.) London: Learning Matters.

Gravells, A. (2012b) *Passing PTLLS Assessments*, (2nd Edn.) London: Learning Matters.

IfL (2009) *Code of Professional Practice: Raising concerns about IfL members* (V2). London: Institute for Learning.

LLUK (2006) *New overarching professional standards for teachers, tutors and trainers in the Lifelong Learning Sector.* London: Skills for Business.

Robinson, K. (2011) *Out of our minds.* Chichester: Capstone Publishing.

Websites

Further Education Teachers' Qualifications (Wales)	http://tiny.cc/o10oc
Institute for Learning	www.ifl.ac.uk
IfL – Code of Professional Practice	www.ifl.ac.uk/professional-standards/code-of-professional-practice
IfL – Professional formation annexe	www.ifl.ac.uk/__data/assets/pdf_file/0015/4641/Professional-Formation-Annexe-A.pdf
IfL – REfLECT	www.ifl.ac.uk/cpd/reflect
LLUK (2009) – The Big Picture	www.slideshare.net/LifelongLearningUK/the-big-picture-1747598
Learning and Skills Improvement Service	www.lsis.org.uk
Microsoft UK Schools – Shift happens	http://blogs.msdn.com/ukschools/archive/2008/09/11/shift-happens-uk-download.aspx
Minimum Core	http://tinyurl.com/315rhvl
Move-on – Skills for Life practice tests	www.move-on.org.uk/practicetests.asp
Ofqual: Explaining the Qualifications and Credit Framework	http://tinyurl.com/447bgy2
Professional Standards for Lecturers in Scotland's colleges	http://tiny.cc/3w9jg
Sector Skills Councils	www.sscalliance.org
Scottish Credit and Qualifications Framework	www.scqf.org.uk
Statutory Instruments 2007 No. 2116 Education England	www.legislation.gov.uk/uksi/2007/2116/pdfs/uksi_20072116_en.pdf
Teaching Qualifications for Northern Ireland	http://tiny.cc/2bexb

APPENDIX I
PTLLS WRITTEN ASSESSMENTS: GUIDANCE

(Relates to the activity in Chapter 1)

PTLLS Level 3 written assessments	
Should have/do:	**Should not have/do:**
Question set out in full as the title unless otherwise instructed.	Spelling errors.
Double- or one-and-a-half-line spacing.	Mistakes in grammar.
Introduction, main body and conclusion well linked.	Mistakes in punctuation.
Acronyms and abbreviations expanded.	Ampersands (use the word *and* in full).
Clear font in 12 pt.	Contractions (such as *it's, isn't*): write words in full, i.e. *it is, is not*.
A clear focus.	Plagiarism – all responses should be in your own words (if any quotations are used, these must be Harvard referenced).
Word count at the end.	Jargon or informal language.
Headers and footers including your name, the date, page number, assessment number, task number and level.	
Note: It is good practice to include a Bibliography set out in the Harvard format showing wider reading.	

PTLLS level 4 written assessments	
Should have/do:	**Should not have/do:**
as level 3, plus:	as level 3, plus:
Use of complete sentences with only minor use of bullets and tables.	Use of inappropriate references which have no provenance. (Provenance refers to origin and authenticity, see Chapter 3.)
Be written in the third person passive, unless you are referring to your own practice, or presenting your own opinions (see Chapter 5 for clarification).	
Evidence of independent reading and research.	
Harvard referencing.	
Analysis and evaluation.	
Demonstrate understanding of the relationship between theory/principles and practice.	
Note: You should check with your PTLLS Award assessor to make sure you are aware of any particular awarding organisation requirements.	

(Relates to the activity in Chapter 5)

Question 1. This is the reference for Gravells' book in John's bibliography. Tick or cross the correct number for each part of this reference in the table below.

<u>Extract from John's assessment</u>

Gravells (2012: 33) states that "it is always useful to get your students to carry out a learning styles test".

1	2	3	4	5	6
Gravells,	A.	(2012)	*Preparing to teach in the lifelong learning sector*, 5th edn.	London	Learning Matters.

	1	2	3	4	5	6
Surname of the writer of the book	☒	☐	☐	☐	☐	☐
Publisher's name	☐	☐	☐	☐	☐	☒
Name of the book	☐	☐	☐	☒	☐	☐
Place of publication...............................	☐	☐	☐	☐	☒	☐
Year of publication	☐	☐	☒	☐	☐	☐
The writer's initial(s)	☐	☒	☐	☐	☐	☐

Question 2. Emma has used the internet to research her assessment. Tick or cross the correct number for each part of the reference in the table below.

1	2	3	4	5	6
Petty,	G.	(2004)	*Active learning* [online]	available at www. geoffpetty.com/ activelearning.html	(accessed 2 June 2012)

	1	2	3	4	5	6
Year of publication on the internet	☐	☐	☒	☐	☐	☐
Author's initials	☐	☒	☐	☐	☐	☐
Website address (URL)	☐	☐	☐	☐	☒	☐
Surname of author	☒	☐	☐	☐	☐	☐

Name of the article .... ☐ ☐ ☐ ☒ ☐ ☐

Date that Emma accessed the internet site ☐ ☐ ☐ ☐ ☐ ☒
....

Question 3. What does '(ed)' mean in this entry in Hasina's References section?

Desforges, C. (ed) (1995) *An introduction to teaching.* Oxford: Blackwell Publishers.

Edition .... ☐

Education .... ☐

Editor .... ☒

Question 4. What does '(edn)' mean in this entry of Ilona's References section?

Gravells, A. (2012) *Preparing to Teach in the Lifelong Learning Sector* (5th edn.), London: Learning Matters.

Edition .... ☒

Education ..... ☐

Editor .... ☐

Question 5. What is the difference between a References section and a Bibliography?

References include only those books, journals, articles, etc., that you have used for quotations and citations .... ☒
....

References will be shorter than a Bibliography .... ☐

A Bibliography includes everything you have read and looked at for the assessment, even if you have not used it for quotations and citations.. ☒

A Bibliography will be a longer list than a Reference list ☐
....

Question 6. A direct quotation of two lines or fewer is encased in quotation marks and remains within the body of the text. How should a direct quotation that is longer than two lines be presented?

In exactly the same format as a shorter one .... ☐

Inset into the text, single-line spaced, without any quotation marks, but preceded by a colon .... ☒

Inset into the text, in the same line spacing as the rest of the text, without quotation marks.. ☐

Encased in quotation marks, inset into the text, in single line spacing ☐
....

(Relates to the activity in Chapter 6)

i	t	r	n	e	d	n	r	c	x	y	x	y	t	a	e	s
p	i	r	d	s	t	e	o	o	i	f	f	e	c	r	e	i
l	a	e	n	i	u	a	l	l	u	i	y	l	l	e	e	t
i	n	l	i	i	s	m	t	i	t	t	y	e	i	v	y	i
a	s	i	a	e	a	c	m	s	v	n	l	n	m	i	e	t
a	s	i	e	v	a	l	u	a	t	e	n	i	f	e	d	i
n	e	s	c	t	a	j	p	s	r	d	r	m	n	w	i	n
r	a	e	e	i	e	n	a	x	s	i	e	a	a	e	e	i
e	r	n	x	s	e	r	a	a	e	l	s	x	p	a	a	c
i	e	n	p	e	t	m	p	l	i	l	e	e	r	m	i	n
i	m	t	l	n	y	u	i	r	y	u	n	l	c	r	o	t
e	c	r	o	t	m	s	e	d	e	s	c	r	i	b	e	c
n	l	c	r	i	t	i	q	u	e	t	e	l	p	m	o	c
c	x	o	e	c	u	d	o	r	p	r	n	y	i	e	y	r
e	s	y	l	a	n	a	y	l	l	a	c	i	t	i	r	c
t	e	s	e	r	u	c	e	t	v	t	e	i	c	r	e	e
w	i	t	i	d	t	r	c	r	s	e	e	t	i	a	t	t

analyse	compare	complete	contrast
critically analyse	critique	define	deliver
describe	discuss	evaluate	examine
explain	explore	identity	illustrate
interpret	justify	list	outline
produce	review	state	summarise

(Relates to the activity in Chapter 6)

To use SMOG

1. Select a text.

2. Count ten sentences.

3. Count the number of words which have three or more syllables.

4. Multiply this by 3.

5. Circle the number closest to your answer.

I	4	9	16	25	36	49	64	81	100	121	144	169

6. Find the square root of the number you circled in the table below:

I	4	9	16	25	36	49	64	81	100	121	144	169
I	2	3	4	5	6	7	8	9	10	11	12	13

7. Add 8 to this total and this will give you the readability level.

A readability level of 10 or below will be understood by most people.

QCF level	Readability level
Entry 3	8–10
Level 1 (broadly equivalent to GCSE grades D–G)	11–15
Level 2 (broadly equivalent to GCSE grades A*–C)	16–20

Books

Buzan, T. (1989) *Use your head*, (2nd edn.) London: BBC Books.

Cottrell, S. (2008) *The Study Skills Handbook*, 3rd edn. Basingstoke: Palgrave Macmillan.

Crystal, D. (2004) *Rediscover grammar*, (3rd edn.) Harlow: Pearson Education.

Gravells, A. (2012a) *Preparing to Teach in the Lifelong Learning Sector*, (5th edn.) London: Learning Matters.

Gravells, A. (2012b) *Passing PTLLS Assessments*, (2nd edn.) London: Learning Matters.

Truss, L. (2003) *Eats, shoots and leaves*. London: Profile Books Limited.

West, C. (2008) *Perfect written English*. London: Random House Books.

Websites

AdultStudent.com (tips for survival and success)	www.adultstudent.com
Alta Visa (search engine)	http://uk.altavista.com
AQA	www.aqa.org.uk
ArmoredPenguin (word puzzles)	www.armoredpenguin.com
Ask Jeeves (search engine)	http://uk.ask.com
BBC/with the Open University (learning styles)	www.open2.net/survey/learningstyles
BeCal (information gateway)	www.becal.net/about_us/need_help.htm
Brainboxx (John Fewings)	www.brainboxx.co.uk
BUBL Information Service (information gateway) — *not updated since April 2011*	http://bubl.ac.uk
Buzan World	www.buzanworld.com/Mind_Maps.htm
CCEA	www.rewardinglearning.org.uk
Citeulike (academic-focused online social bookmarking tool)	www.citeulike.org
City & Guilds	www.cityandguilds.com
Connotea (academic-focused online social bookmarking tool)	www.connotea.org
Delicious (online social bookmarking tool)	http://delicious.com

Department for Business, Innovation and Skills	www.bis.gov.uk
Department for Education	www.education.gov.uk
Digital Unite, Learning Zone	http://learning.digitalunite.com
Diigo (online social bookmarking tool)	www.diigo.com
Edexcel	www.edexcel.com
EndNote Web	www.endnote.com
ESCalate (resources for post-16 education) – *not updated since 31/12/2011*	http://escalate.ac.uk
Eurydice, NFER (information gateway)	www.nfer.ac.uk/eurydice
Excellence Gateway (LSIS) (information gateway)	www.excellencegateway.org.uk
Excellence Gateway (LSIS) (professional standards, England)	www.excellencegateway.org.uk/page. aspx?o=320923
Find Articles (articles in magazines, journals, trade publications and newspapers)	http://findarticles.com
Further Education Teachers' Qualifications (England) Regulations 2007	www.legislation.gov.uk/uksi/2007/2264/ contents/made
Further Education Teachers' Qualifications (Wales)	http://tiny.cc/o10oc
Go on, make online easy	http://learn.go-on.co.uk
Google (search engine)	www.google.co.uk
Google Books NGram Viewer	http://books.google.com/ngrams
Google e-bookstore	http://books.google.com/ebooks?uid=11752200 4192189783614&as_coll=1040
Google Scholar (search engine)	http://scholar.google.co.uk
Gravells, Ann (resources and information about teaching)	www.anngravells.co.uk
H20 Playlist (academic-focused online social bookmarking tool)	http://h2obeta.law.harvard.edu
Hathui Trust (e-books)	www.hathitrust.org
IngentaConnect (online journal abstracts and articles)	www.ingentaconnect.com
Institute for Learning	www.ifl.ac.uk
Intute (information gateway) – *not updated since July 2011*	www.intute.ac.uk

Learning and Skills Network	www.lsneducation.org.uk
LibraryThing (books-focused online social bookmarking tool)	www.librarything.com
Maslow, Abraham	http://maslow.com
Microsoft Digital Literacy Curriculum	www.microsoft.com/uk/education/schools/curriculum-resources/digital-literacy-curriculum.aspx)
Move on Skills for Life practice tests	www.move-on.org.uk/practicetests.asp
NIACE	www.niace.org.uk
OCR	www.ocr.org.uk
Open Library	http://openlibrary.org
Open Office (free software)	http://download.openoffice.org http://templates.services.openoffice.org/en/node/3247
Open University Learning Space (free online resources)	http://openlearn.open.ac.uk
Palgrave Study Skills (Skills4Study)	www.skills4study.com
PCET	www.pcet.net
Petty	www.geoffpetty.com/activelearning.html
Pinakes (links to major information gateways)	www.hw.ac.uk/libwww/irn/pinakes/pinakes.html
Plagiarism	www.plagiarism.org/plag_article_what_is_plagiarism.html
Plagiarism – JCQ	www.jcq.org.uk/attachments/published/672/Plagiarism%20in%20Examinations%20FINAL.pdf
Plagiarism Checker	www.dustball.com/cs/plagiarism.checker
Plagiarism Checker	www.plagiarismchecker.com
Project Gutenberg	www.gutenberg.org
Questia (online library: search free, but subscription to access)	www.questia.com
Scottish Credit and Qualifications Framework	www.scqf.org.uk
SQA	www.sqa.org.uk
Teaching Qualifications for Northern Ireland	http://tiny.cc/2bexb
TEC (learning styles)	http://tecweb.org
TES Online	www.tes.co.uk
Turnitin	www.turnitin.com

VARK (Neil Fleming)	www.vark-learn.com
Wikipedia	www.wikipedia.org
Williams, Jacklyn (resources and information about teaching)	www.prosolteaching.co.uk
WJEC	www.wjec.co.uk
Wordle	www.wordle.net
WriteCheck	https://www.writecheck.com/static/home.html (note that the s in the http part of the address indicates a secure site.)
Yahoo! (search engine)	http://m.uk.yahoo.com